BY BERTRAND RUSSELL

AUTHORITY AND THE INDIVIDUAL
HUMAN KNOWLEDGE: ITS SCOPE AND LIMITS
HISTORY OF WESTERN PHILOSOPHY
THE PRINCIPLES OF MATHEMATICS
INTRODUCTION TO MATHEMATICAL PHILOSOPHY
THE ANALYSIS OF MIND
OUR KNOWLEDGE OF THE EXTERNAL WORLD
AN OUTLINE OF PHILOSOPHY
THE PHILOSOPHY OF LEIBNIZ
AN INQUIRY INTO MEANING AND TRUTH

POWER
IN PRAISE OF IDLENESS
THE CONQUEST OF HAPPINESS
SKEPTICAL ESSAYS
MYSTICISM AND LOGIC
THE SCIENTIFIC OUTLOOK
MARRIAGE AND MORALS
EDUCATION AND THE SOCIAL ORDER
ON EDUCATION

FREEDOM AND ORGANIZATION, 1814–1914
PRINCIPLES OF SOCIAL RECONSTRUCTION
ROADS TO FREEDOM
JUSTICE IN WAR-TIME
FREE THOUGHT AND OFFICIAL PROPAGANDA
THE PROBLEM OF CHINA

BERTRAND RUSSELL

UNPOPULAR ESSAYS

SIMON AND SCHUSTER

NEW YORK

MANUFACTURED IN THE UNITED STATES OF AMERICA
BY H. WOLFF BOOK MFG. CO., NEW YORK

PREFACE

MOST of the following essays, which were written at various times during the last fifteen years, are concerned to combat, in one way or another, the growth of dogmatism, whether of the Right or of the Left, which has hitherto characterized our tragic century. This serious purpose inspires them even if, at times, they seem flippant, for those who are solemn and pontifical are not to be successfully fought by being even more solemn and even more pontifical.

A word as to the title. In the Preface to my *Human Knowledge* I said that I was writing not only for professional philosophers, and that "philosophy proper deals with matters of interest to the general educated public." Reviewers took me to task, saying they found parts of the book difficult, and implying that my words were such as to mislead purchasers. I do not wish to expose myself again to this charge; I will therefore confess that there are several sentences in the present volume which some unusually stupid children of ten might find a little puzzling. On this ground I do not claim that the essays are popular; and if not popular, then "unpopular."

BERTRAND RUSSELL

April, 1950

ACKNOWLEDGMENT

Three of the essays included in this volume—*An Outline of Intellectual Rubbish, Ideas That Have Helped Mankind,* and *Ideas That Have Harmed Mankind*—were originally published by Mr. E. Haldeman-Julius of Girard, Kansas, with whose permission they are now reprinted.

B. R.

CONTENTS

CHAPTER   PAGE

Preface   V

I. *Philosophy and Politics*   I

II. *Philosophy for Laymen*   21

III. *The Future of Mankind*   34

IV. *Philosophy's Ulterior Motives*   45

V. *The Superior Virtue of the Oppressed*   58

VI. *On Being Modern-minded*   65

VII. *An Outline of Intellectual Rubbish*   71

VIII. *The Functions of a Teacher*   112

IX. *Ideas That Have Helped Mankind*   124

X. *Ideas That Have Harmed Mankind*   146

XI. *Eminent Men I Have Known*   166

XII. *Obituary*   173

UNPOPULAR ESSAYS

Philosophy and Politics

THE British are distinguished among the nations of modern Europe, on the one hand by the excellence of their philosophers, and on the other hand by their contempt for philosophy. In both respects they show their wisdom. But contempt for philosophy, if developed to the point at which it becomes systematic, is itself a philosophy; it is the philosophy which, in America, is called "instrumentalism." I shall suggest that philosophy, if it is bad philosophy, may be dangerous, and therefore deserves that degree of negative respect which we accord to lightning and tigers. What positive respect may be due to "good" philosophy I will leave for the moment an open question.

The connection of philosophy with politics, which is the subject of my lecture, has been less evident in Britain than in Continental countries. Empiricism, broadly speaking, is connected with liberalism, but Hume was a Tory; what philosophers call "idealism" has, in general, a similar connection with conservatism, but T. H. Green was a Liberal. On the Continent distinctions have been more clear cut, and there has been a greater readiness to accept or reject a block of doctrines as a whole, without critical scrutiny of each separate part.

In most civilized countries at most times, philosophy has

been a matter in which the authorities had an official opinion, and except where liberal democracy prevails this is still the case. The Catholic Church is connected to the philosophy of Aquinas, the Soviet government to that of Marx. The Nazis upheld German idealism, though the degree of allegiance to be given to Kant, Fichte, or Hegel respectively was not clearly laid down. Catholics, Communists, and Nazis all consider that their views on practical politics are bound up with their views on theoretical philosophy. Democratic liberalism, in its early successes, was connected with the empirical philosophy developed by Locke. I want to consider this relation of philosophies to political systems as it has in fact existed, and to inquire how far it is a valid logical relation, and how far, even if not logical, it has a kind of psychological inevitability. In so far as either kind of relation exists, a man's philosophy has practical importance, and a prevalent philosophy may have an intimate connection with the happiness or misery of large sections of mankind.

The word "philosophy" is one of which the meaning is by no means fixed. Like the word "religion," it has one sense when used to describe certain features of historical cultures, and another when used to denote a study or an attitude of mind which is considered desirable in the present day. Philosophy, as pursued in the universities of the Western democratic world, is, at least in intention, part of the pursuit of knowledge, aiming at the same kind of detachment as is sought in science, and not required by the authorities to arrive at conclusions convenient to the government. Many teachers of philosophy would repudiate not only the intention to influence their pupils' politics but also the view that philosophy should inculcate virtue. This, they would say, has as little to do with the philosopher as with the physicist or the chemist. Knowledge, they would say, should be the sole purpose of university teaching; virtue should be left to parents, schoolmasters, and churches.

But this view of philosophy, with which I have much sympathy, is very modern, and even in the modern world exceptional. There is a quite different view, which has prevailed since antiquity, and to which philosophy has owed its social and political importance.

Philosophy, in this historically usual sense, has resulted from the attempt to produce a synthesis of science and religion, or, perhaps more exactly, to combine a doctrine as to the nature of the universe and man's place in it with a practical ethic inculcating what was considered the best way of life. Philosophy was distinguished from religion by the fact that, nominally at least, it did not appeal to authority or tradition; it was distinguished from science by the fact that an essential part of its purpose was to tell men how to live. Its cosmological and ethical theories were closely interconnected: sometimes ethical motives influenced the philosopher's views as to the nature of the universe, sometimes his views as to the universe led him to ethical conclusions. And with most philosophers ethical opinions involved political consequences: some valued democracy, others oligarchy; some praised liberty, others discipline. Almost all types of philosophy were invented by the Greeks, and the controversies of our own day were already vigorous among the pre-Socratics.

The fundamental problem of ethics and politics is that of finding some way of reconciling the needs of social life with the urgency of individual desires. This has been achieved, in so far as it has been achieved, by means of various devices. Where a government exists, the criminal law can be used to prevent anti-social action on the part of those who do not belong to the government, and law can be reinforced by religion wherever religion teaches that disobedience is impiety. Where there is a priesthood sufficiently influential to enforce its moral code on lay rulers, even the rulers become to some extent subject to law; of this there are abundant instances in the Old Testament and in medieval history. Kings who genuinely believe in the Divine government of the world, and in a system of rewards and punishments in the next life, feel themselves not omnipotent, and not able to sin with impunity. This feeling is expressed by the King in *Hamlet*, when he contrasts the inflexibility of Divine justice with the subservience of earthly judges to the royal power.

Philosophers, when they have tackled the problem of preserving social coherence, have sought solutions less obviously dependent upon dogma than those offered by official religions. Most philosophy has been a reaction against skepticism; it has arisen in ages when authority no longer sufficed to produce the socially necessary minimum of belief, so that nominally rational arguments had to be invented to secure the same result. This motive has led to a deep insincerity infecting most philosophy, both ancient and modern. There has been a fear, often unconscious, that clear thinking would lead to anarchy, and this fear has led philosophers to hide in mists of fallacy and obscurity.

There have, of course, been exceptions; the most notable are Protagoras in antiquity, and Hume in modern times. Both, as a result of skepticism, were politically conservative. Protagoras did not know whether the gods exist, but he held that in any case they ought to be worshiped. Philosophy, according to him, had nothing edifying to teach, and for the survival of morals we must rely upon the thoughtlessness of the majority and their willingness to believe what they had been taught. Nothing, therefore, must be done to weaken the popular force of tradition.

The same sort of thing, up to a point, may be said about Hume. After setting forth his skeptical conclusions, which, he admits, are not such as men can live by, he passes on to a piece of practical advice which, if followed, would prevent anybody from reading him. "Carelessness and inattention," he says, "alone can afford us any remedy. For this reason I rely entirely upon them." He does not, in this connection, set forth his reasons for being a Tory, but it is obvious that "carelessness and inattention," while they may lead to acquiescence in the *status quo*, cannot, unaided, lead a man to advocate this or that scheme of reform.

Hobbes, though less skeptical than Hume, was equally persuaded that government is not of divine origin, and was equally led, by the road of disbelief, to advocacy of extreme conservatism.

Protagoras was "answered" by Plato, and Hume by Kant and Hegel. In each case the philosophical world heaved a sigh of relief, and refrained from examining too nicely the intellectual validity of the "answer," which in each case had political as well as theoretical consequences—though in the case of the "answer" to Hume it was not the Liberal Kant but the reactionary Hegel who developed the *political* consequences.

But thorough-going skeptics, such as Protagoras and Hume, have never been influential, and have served chiefly as bugbears to be used by reactionaries in frightening people into irrational dogmatism. The really powerful adversaries against whom Plato and Hegel had to contend were not skeptics, but empiricists, Democritus in the one case and Locke in the other. In each case empiricism was associated with democracy and with a more or less utilitarian ethic. In each case the new philosophy succeeded in presenting itself as nobler and more profound than the philosophy of pedestrian common sense which it superseded. In each case, in the name of all that was most sublime, the new philosophy made itself the champion of injustice, cruelty, and opposition to progress. In the case of Hegel this has come to be more or less recognized; in the case of Plato it is still something of a paradox, though it has been brilliantly advocated in a recent book by Dr. K. R. Popper.[1]

Plato, according to Diogenes Laertius, expressed the view

[1] *The Open Society and its Enemies.* The same thesis is maintained in my *History of Western Philosophy.*

that all the books of Democritus ought to be burned. His wish was so far fulfilled that none of the writings of Democritus survive. Plato, in his Dialogues, never mentioned him; Aristotle gave some account of his doctrines; Epicurus vulgarized him; and finally Lucretius put the doctrines of Epicurus into verse. Lucretius just survived, by a happy accident. To reconstruct Democritus from the controversy of Aristotle and the poetry of Lucretius is not easy; it is almost as if we had to reconstruct Plato from Locke's refutation of innate ideas and Vaughan's "I saw eternity the other night." Nevertheless enough can be done to explain and condemn Plato's hatred.

Democritus is chiefly famous as (along with Leucippus) the founder of atomism, which he advocated in spite of the objections of metaphysicians—objections which were repeated by their successors down to and including Descartes and Leibniz. His atomism, however, was only part of his general philosophy. He was a materialist, a determinist, a free thinker, a utilitarian who disliked all strong passions, a believer in evolution, both astronomical and biological.

Like the men of similar opinions in the eighteenth century, Democritus was an ardent democrat. "Poverty in a democracy," he says, "is as much to be preferred to what is called prosperity under despots as freedom is to slavery." He was a contemporary of Socrates and Protagoras, and a fellow-townsman of the latter; he flourished during the early years of the Peloponnesian war, but may have died before it ended. That war concentrated the struggle that was taking place throughout the Hellenic world between democracy and oligarchy. Sparta stood for oligarchy; so did Plato's family and friends, who were thus led to become Quislings. Their treachery is held to have contributed to the defeat of Athens. After that defeat, Plato set to work to sing the praises of the victors by constructing a Utopia of which the main features were suggested by the constitution of Sparta. Such, however, was his artistic skill that Liberals never noticed his reactionary tendencies until his disciples Lenin and Hitler had supplied them with a practical exegesis.[1]

That Plato's Republic should have been admired, on its political side, by decent people is perhaps the most astonishing example of literary snobbery in all history. Let us consider a few points in this totalitarian tract. The main purpose of education, to which everything else is subordinated, is to produce courage in battle. To this end, there is to be a rigid censorship of the stories told by mothers and nurses to young children; there is to be no reading of Homer, because that degraded versifier makes heroes lament and gods laugh; the drama is to be forbidden, because it contains villains and women; music is to be only of certain kinds, which, in modern terms, would be "Rule Britannia" and "The British Grenadiers." The government is to be in the hands of a small oligarchy, who are to practice trickery and lying—trickery in manipulating the drawing of lots for eugenic purposes, and elaborate lying to persuade the population that there are biological differences between the upper and lower classes. Finally, there is to be a large-scale infanticide when children are born otherwise than as a result of governmental swindling in the drawing of lots.

Whether people are happy in this community does not matter, we are told, for excellence resides in the whole, not in the parts. Plato's city is a copy of the eternal city laid up in heaven; perhaps in heaven we shall enjoy the kind of existence it offers us, but if we do not enjoy it here on earth, so much the worse for us.

This system derives its persuasive force from the marriage of aristocratic prejudice and "divine philosophy"; without the latter, its repulsiveness would be obvious. The fine talk about the good and the unchanging makes it possible to lull the reader

[1] In 1920 I compared the Soviet State to Plato's Republic, to the equal indignation of Communists and Platonists.

into acquiescence in the doctrine that the wise should rule, and that their purpose should be to preserve the *status quo,* as the ideal state in heaven does. To every man of strong political convictions—and the Greeks had amazingly vehement political passions—it is obvious that "the good" are those of his own party, and that, if they could establish the constitution they desire, no further change would be necessary. So Plato thought, but by concealing his thought in a metaphysical mist he gave it an impersonal and disinterested appearance which deceived the world for ages.

The ideal of static perfection, which Plato derived from Parmenides and embodied in his theory of ideas, is one which is now generally recognized as inapplicable to human affairs. Man is a restless animal, not content, like the boa constrictor, to have a good meal once a month and sleep the rest of the time. Man needs, for his happiness, not only the enjoyment of this or that, but hope and enterprise and change. As Hobbes says, "Felicity consisteth in prospering, not in having prospered." Among modern philosophers, the ideal of unending and unchanging bliss has been replaced by that of evolution, in which there is supposed to be an orderly progress toward a goal which is never quite attained or at any rate has not been attained at the time of writing. This change of outlook is part of the substitution of dynamics for statics which began with Galileo, and which has increasingly affected all modern thinking, whether scientific or political.

Change is one thing, progress is another. "Change" is scientific, "progress" is ethical; change is indubitable, whereas progress is a matter of controversy. Let us first consider change, as it appears in science.

Until the time of Galileo, astronomers, following Aristotle, believed that everything in the heavens, from the moon upwards, is unchanging and incorruptible. Since Laplace, no reputable astronomer has held this view. Nebulae stars, and planets, we now believe, have all developed gradually. Some stars, for instance, the companion of Sirius, are "dead"; they have at some time undergone a cataclysm which has enormously diminished the amount of light and heat radiating from them. Our own planet, in which philosophers are apt to take a parochial and excessive interest, was once too hot to support life, and will in time be too cold. After ages during which the earth produced harmless trilobites and butterflies, evolution progressed to the point at which it generated Neros, Genghis Khans, and Hitlers. This, however, is a passing nightmare; in time the earth will become again incapable of supporting life, and peace will return.

But this purposeless see-saw, which is all that science has to offer, has not satisfied the philosophers. They have professed to discover a formula of progress, showing that the world was becoming gradually more and more to their liking. The recipe for a philosophy of this type is simple. The philosopher first decides which are the features of the existing world that give him pleasure, and which are the features that give him pain. He then, by a careful selection among facts, persuades himself that the universe is subject to a general law leading to an increase of what he finds pleasant and a decrease of what he finds unpleasant. Next, having formulated his law of progress, he turns on the public and says: "It is fated that the world must develop as I say; therefore those who wish to be on the winning side, and do not care to wage a fruitless war against the inevitable, will join my party." Those who oppose him are condemned as unphilosophic, unscientific, and out of date, while those who agree with him feel assured of victory, since the universe is on their side. At the same time the winning side, for reasons which remain somewhat obscure, is represented as the side of virtue.

The man who first fully developed this point of view was Hegel. Hegel's philosophy is so odd that one would not have expected him to be able to get sane men to accept it, but he did. He set it out with so much obscurity that people thought it must be profound. It can quite easily be expounded lucidly in words of one syllable, but then its absurdity becomes obvious. What follows is not a caricature, though of course Hegelians will maintain that it is.

Hegel's philosophy, in outline, is as follows. Real reality is timeless, as in Parmenides and Plato, but there is also an apparent reality, consisting of the every-day world in space and time. The character of real reality can be determined by logic alone, since there is only one sort of possible reality that is not self-contradictory. This is called the "Absolute Idea." Of this he gives the following definition: *"The Absolute Idea.* The idea, as unity of the subjective and objective Idea, is the notion of the Idea—a notion whose objective is the Idea as such, and for which the objective is Idea—an Object which embraces all characteristics in its unity." I hate to spoil the luminous clarity of this sentence by any commentary, but in fact the same thing would be expressed by saying "The Absolute Idea is pure thought thinking about pure thought." Hegel has already proved to his satisfaction that all Reality is thought, from which it follows that thought cannot think about anything but thought, since there is nothing else to think about. Some people might find this a little dull; they might say: "I like thinking about Cape Horn and the South Pole and Mount Everest and the great nebula in Andromeda; I enjoy contemplating the ages when the earth was cooling while the sea boiled and volcanoes rose and fell between night and morning. I find your precept, that I should fill my mind with the lucubrations of word-spinning professors, intolerably stuffy, and really, if that is your 'happy ending,' I don't think it was worth while to wade through all the verbiage that led up to it." And with these words they would say goodbye to philosophy and live happy ever after.

But if we agreed with these people we should be doing Hegel an injustice, which God forbid. For Hegel would point out that, while the Absolute, like Aristotle's God, never thinks about anything but itself, because it knows that all else is illusion, yet we, who are forced to live in the world of phenomena, as slaves of the temporal process, seeing only the parts, and only dimly apprehending the whole in moments of mystic insight, we, illusory products of illusion, are compelled to think as though Cape Horn were self-subsistent and not merely an idea in the Divine Mind. When we think we think about Cape Horn, what happens in Reality is that the Absolute is aware of a Cape-Horny thought. It really does have such a thought, or rather such an aspect of the one thought that it timelessly thinks and is, and this is the only reality that belongs to Cape Horn. But since we cannot reach such heights, we are doing our best in thinking of it in the ordinary geographical way.

But what, someone may say, has all this to do with politics? At first sight, perhaps, not very much. To Hegel, however, the connection is obvious. It follows from his metaphysic that true liberty consists in obedience to an arbitrary authority, that free speech is an evil, that absolute monarchy is good, that the Prussian State was the best existing at the time when he wrote, that war is good, and that an international organization for the peaceful settlement of disputes would be a misfortune.

It is just possible that some among my readers may not see at once how these consequences follow, so I hope I may be pardoned for saying a few words about the intermediate steps.

Although time is unreal, the series of appearances which constitutes history has a curious relation to Reality. Hegel discovered the nature of Reality by a purely logical process called the "dialectic," which consists of discovering contradictions in abstract ideas and correcting them by making them less abstract. Each of these abstract ideas is conceived as a stage in the development of "The Idea," the last stage being the "Absolute Idea."

Oddly enough, for some reason which Hegel never divulged, the temporal process of history repeats the logical development of the dialectic. It might be thought, since the metaphysic professes to apply to all Reality, that the temporal process which parallels it would be cosmic, but not a bit of it: it is purely terrestrial, confined to recorded history, and (incredible as this may seem) to the history that Hegel happened to know. Different nations, at different times, have embodied the stages of the Idea that the dialectic had reached at those times. Of China, Hegel knew only that it *was*, therefore China illustrated the category of mere Being. Of India he knew only that Buddhists believed in Nirvana, therefore India illustrated the category of nothing. The Greeks and Romans got rather further along the list of categories, but all the late stages have been left to the Germans, who, since the time of the fall of Rome, have been the sole standard-bearers of the Idea, and had already in 1830 very nearly realized the Absolute Idea.

To anyone who still cherishes the hope that man is a more or less rational animal, the success of this farrago of nonsense must be astonishing. In his own day, his system was accepted by almost all academically educated young Germans, which is perhaps explicable by the fact that it flattered German self-esteem. What is more surprising is its success outside Germany. When I was young, most teachers of philosophy in British and American universities were Hegelians, so that, until I read Hegel, I supposed there must be some truth in his system; I was cured, however, by discovering that everything he said on the philosophy of mathematics was plain nonsense.

Most curious of all was his effect on Marx, who took over some of his most fanciful tenets, more particularly the belief that history develops according to a logical plan, and is concerned, like the purely abstract dialectic, to find ways of avoiding self-contradiction. Over a large part of the earth's surface you will be liquidated if you question this dogma, and eminent Western men of science, who sympathize politically with Russia, show their sympathy by using the word "contradiction" in ways that no self-respecting logician can approve.

In tracing a connection between the politics and the metaphysics of a man like Hegel, we must content ourselves with certain very general features of his practical program. That Hegel glorified Prussia was something of an accident; in his earlier years he ardently admired Napoleon, and only became a German patriot when he became an employee of the Prussian State. Even in the latest form of his Philosophy of History, he still mentions Alexander, Caesar, and Napoleon as men great enough to have a right to consider themselves exempt from the obligations of the moral law. What his philosophy constrained him to admire was not Germany as against France, but order, system, regulation, and intensity of governmental control. His deification of the state would have been just as shocking if the state concerned had been Napoleon's despotism. In his own opinion, he knew what the world needed, though most men did not; a strong government might compel men to act for the best, which democracy could never do. Heraclitus, to whom Hegel was deeply indebted, says: "Every beast is driven to the pasture with blows." Let us, in any case, make sure of the blows; whether they lead to a pasture is a matter of minor importance—except, of course, to the "beasts."

It is obvious that an autocratic system, such as that advocated by Hegel or by Marx's present-day disciples, is only theoretically justifiable on a basis of unquestioned dogma. If you know for certain what is the purpose of the universe in relation to human life, what is going to happen, and what is good for people even if they do not think so; if you can say, as Hegel does, that his theory of history is "a result which happens to

be known to *me*, because I have traversed the entire field"—
then you will feel that no degree of coercion is too great,
provided it leads to the goal.

The only philosophy that affords a theoretical justification
of democracy, and that accords with democracy in its temper
of mind, is empiricism. Locke, who may be regarded, so far as
the modern world is concerned, as the founder of empiricism,
makes it clear how closely this is connected with his views on
liberty and toleration, and with his opposition to absolute
monarchy. He is never tired of emphasizing the uncertainty of
most of our knowledge, not with a skeptical intention such as
Hume's, but with the intention of making men aware that they
may be mistaken, and that they should take account of this
possibility in all their dealings with men of opinions different
from their own. He had seen the evils wrought, both by the
"enthusiasm" of the sectaries, and by the dogma of the divine
right of kings; to both he opposed a piecemeal and patch-
work political doctrine, to be tested at each point by its success
in practice.

What may be called, in a broad sense, the Liberal theory of
politics is a recurrent product of commerce. The first known
example of it was in the Ionian cities of Asia Minor, which lived
by trading with Egypt and Lydia. When Athens, in the time
of Pericles, became commercial, the Athenians became Liberal.
After a long eclipse, Liberal ideas revived in the Lombard cities
of the middle ages, and prevailed in Italy until they were
extinguished by the Spaniards in the sixteenth century. But the
Spaniards failed to reconquer Holland or to subdue England,
and it was these countries that were the champions of Liberalism and the leaders in commerce in the seventeenth century.
In our day the leadership has passed to the United States.

The reasons for the connection of commerce with Liberalism are obvious. Trade brings men into contact with tribal
customs different from their own, and in so doing destroys the

dogmatism of the untraveled. The relation of buyer and seller is one of negotiation between two parties who are both free; it is most profitable when the buyer or seller is able to understand the point of view of the other party. There is, of course, imperialistic commerce, where men are forced to buy at the point of the sword; but this is not the kind that generates Liberal philosophies, which have flourished best in trading cities that have wealth without much military strength. In the present day, the nearest analogue to the commercial cities of antiquity and the middle ages is to be found in small countries such as Switzerland, Holland, and Scandinavia.

The Liberal creed, in practice, is one of live-and-let-live, of toleration and freedom so far as public order permits, of moderation and absence of fanaticism in political programs. Even democracy, when it becomes fanatical, as it did among Rousseau's disciples in the French Revolution, ceases to be Liberal; indeed, a fanatical belief in democracy makes democratic institutions impossible, as appeared in England under Cromwell and in France under Robespierre. The genuine Liberal does not say "this is true," he says "I am inclined to think that under present circumstances this opinion is probably the best." And it is only in this limited and undogmatic sense that he will advocate democracy.

What has theoretical philosophy to say that is relevant to the validity or otherwise of the Liberal outlook?

The essence of the Liberal outlook lies not in *what* opinions are held, but in *how* they are held: instead of being held dogmatically, they are held tentatively, and with a consciousness that new evidence may at any moment lead to their abandonment. This is the way in which opinions are held in science, as opposed to the way in which they are held in theology. The decisions of the Council of Nicaea are still authoritative, but in science fourth-century opinions no longer carry any weight. In the U.S.S.R. the dicta of Marx on dialectical materialism are so unquestioned that they help to determine the views of geneticists on how to obtain the best breed of wheat,[1] though elsewhere it is thought that experiment is the right way to study such problems. Science is empirical, tentative, and undogmatic; all immutable dogma is unscientific. The scientific outlook, accordingly, is the intellectual counterpart of what is, in the practical sphere, the outlook of Liberalism.

Locke, who first developed in detail the empiricist theory of knowledge, preached also religious toleration, representative institutions, and the limitation of governmental power by the system of checks and balances. Few of his doctrines were new, but he developed them in a weighty manner at just the moment when the English government was prepared to accept them. Like the other men of 1688, he was only reluctantly a rebel, and he disliked anarchy as much as he disliked despotism. Both in intellectual and in practical matters he stood for order without authority; this might be taken as the motto both of science and of Liberalism. It depends, clearly, upon consent or assent. In the intellectual world it involves standards of evidence which, after adequate discussion, will lead to a measure of agreement among experts. In the practical world it involves submission to the majority after all parties have had an opportunity to state their case.

In both respects his moment was a fortunate one. The great controversy between the Ptolemaic and Copernican systems had been decided, and scientific questions could no longer be settled by an appeal to Aristotle. Newton's triumphs seemed to justify boundless scientific optimism.

In the practical world, a century and a half of wars of religion had produced hardly any change in the balance of power as between Protestants and Catholics. Enlightened men had

---

[1] See *The New Genetics in the Soviet Union*, by Hudson and Richens. School of Agriculture, Cambridge, 1946.

begun to view theological controversies as an absurdity, caricatured in Swift's war between the Big-endians and the Little-endians. The extreme Protestant sects, by relying upon the inner light, had made what professed to be Revelation into an anarchic force. Delightful enterprises, scientific and commercial, invited energetic men to turn aside from barren disputation. Fortunately they accepted the invitation, and two centuries of unexampled progress resulted.

We are now again in an epoch of wars of religion, but a religion is now called an "ideology." At the moment, the Liberal philosophy is felt by many to be too tame and middle-aged: the idealistic young look for something with more bite in it, something which has a definite answer to all their questions, which calls for missionary activity and gives hope of a millennium brought about by conquest. In short, we have been plunging into a renewed age of faith. Unfortunately the atomic bomb is a swifter exterminator than the stake, and cannot safely be allowed so long a run. We must hope that a more rational outlook can be made to prevail, for only through a revival of Liberal tentativeness and tolerance can our world survive.

The empiricist's theory of knowledge—to which, with some reservations, I adhere—is halfway between dogma and skepticism. Almost all knowledge, it holds, is in some degree doubtful, though the doubt, if any, is negligible as regards pure mathematics and facts of present sense-perception. The doubtfulness of what passes for knowledge is a matter of degree; having recently read a book on the Anglo-Saxon invasion of Britain, I am now convinced of the existence of Hengist, but very doubtful about Horsa. Einstein's general theory of relativity is probably broadly speaking true, but when it comes to calculating the circumference of the universe we may be pardoned for expecting later investigations to give a somewhat different result. The modern theory of the atom has pragmatic truth, since it enables us to construct atomic bombs: its consequences are what instrumentalists facetiously call "satisfactory." But it is not improbable that some quite different theory may in time be found to give a better explanation of the observed facts. Scientific theories are accepted as useful hypotheses to suggest further research, and as having some element of truth in virtue of which they are able to colligate existing observations; but no sensible person regards them as immutably perfect.

In the sphere of practical politics, this intellectual attitude has important consequences. In the first place, it is not worth while to inflict a comparatively certain present evil for the sake of a comparatively doubtful future good. If the theology of former times was entirely correct, it was worth while burning a number of people at the stake in order that the survivors might go to heaven, but if it was doubtful whether heretics would go to hell, the argument for persecution was not valid. If it is certain that Marx's eschatology is true, and that as soon as private capitalism has been abolished we shall all be happy ever after, then it is right to pursue this end by means of dictatorships, concentration camps, and world wars; but if the end is doubtful or the means not sure to achieve it, present misery becomes an irresistible argument against such drastic methods. If it were certain that without Jews the world would be a paradise, there could be no valid objection to Auschwitz; but if it is much more probable that the world resulting from such methods would be a hell, we can allow free play to our natural humanitarian revulsion against cruelty.

Since, broadly speaking, the distant consequences of actions are more uncertain than the immediate consequences, it is seldom justifiable to embark on any policy on the ground that, though harmful in the present, it will be beneficial in the long run. This principle, like all others held by empiricists, must not be held absolutely; there are cases where the future consequences of one policy are fairly certain and very unpleasant, while the present consequences of the other, though not agreeable, are easily endurable. This applies, for instance, to saving food for the winter, investing capital in machinery, and so on. But even in such cases uncertainty should not be lost sight of. During a boom there is much investment that turns out to have been unprofitable, and modern economists recognize that the habit of investing rather than consuming may easily be carried too far.

It is commonly urged that, in a war between Liberals and fanatics, the fanatics are sure to win, owing to their more unshakable belief in the righteousness of their cause. This belief dies hard, although all history, including that of the last few years, is against it. Fanatics have failed, over and over again, because they have attempted the impossible, or because, even when what they aimed at was possible, they were too unscientific to adopt the right means; they have failed also because they roused the hostility of those whom they wished to coerce. In every important war since 1700 the more democratic side has been victorious. This is partly because democracy and empiricism (which are intimately interconnected) do not demand a distortion of facts in the interests of theory. Russia and Canada, which have somewhat similar climatic conditions, are both interested in obtaining better breeds of wheat; in Canada this aim is pursued experimentally, in Russia by interpreting the Marxist Scriptures.

Systems of dogma without empirical foundation, such as those of scholastic theology, Marxism, and fascism, have the advantage of producing a great degree of social coherence among their disciples. But they have the disadvantage of involving persecution of valuable sections of the population. Spain was ruined by the expulsion of the Jews and Moors; France suffered by the emigration of Huguenots after the Revocation of the Edict of Nantes; Germany would probably have been first in the field with the atomic bomb but for Hitler's hatred of Jews. And, to repeat, dogmatic systems have the two further disadvantages of involving false beliefs on practically important matters of fact, and of rousing violent hostility in those who do not share the fanaticism in question. For these various reasons, it is not to be expected that, in the long run, nations addicted to a dogmatic philosophy will have the advantage over those of a more empirical temper. Nor is it true that dogma is necessary for social coherence when social coherence is called for; no nation could have shown more of it than the British showed in 1940.

Empiricism, finally, is to be commended not only on the ground of its greater truth, but also on ethical grounds. Dogma demands authority, rather than intelligent thought, as the source of opinion; it requires persecution of heretics and hostility to unbelievers; it asks of its disciples that they should inhibit natural kindliness in favor of systematic hatred. Since argument is not recognized as a means of arriving at truth, adherents of rival dogmas have no method except war by means of which to reach a decision. And war, in our scientific age, means, sooner or later, universal death.

I conclude that, in our day as in the time of Locke, empiricist Liberalism (which is not incompatible with *democratic* socialism) is the only philosophy that can be adopted by a man who, on the one hand, demands some scientific evidence for his beliefs, and, on the other hand, desires human happiness more than the prevalence of this or that party or creed. Our confused and difficult world needs various things if it is to escape disaster, and among these one of the most necessary is that, in the nations which still uphold Liberal beliefs, these beliefs should be whole-hearted and profound, not apologetic towards dogmatisms of the right and of the left, but deeply persuaded of the value of liberty, scientific freedom, and mutual forbearance. For without these beliefs life on our politically divided but technically unified planet will hardly continue to be possible.

Philosophy for Laymen

M ANKIND, ever since there have been civilized communities, have been confronted with problems of two different kinds. On the one hand there has been the problem of mastering natural forces, of acquiring the knowledge and the skill required to produce tools and weapons and to encourage Nature in the production of useful animals and plants. This problem, in the modern world, is dealt with by science and scientific technique, and experience has shown that in order to deal with it adequately it is necessary to train a large number of rather narrow specialists.

But there is a second problem, less precise, and by some mistakenly regarded as unimportant—I mean the problem of how best to utilize our command over the forces of nature. This includes such burning issues as democracy versus dictatorship, capitalism versus socialism, international government versus international anarchy, free speculation versus authoritarian dogma. On such issues the laboratory can give no decisive guidance. The kind of knowledge that gives most help in solving such problems is a wide survey of human life, in the past as well as in the present, and an appreciation of the sources of misery or contentment as they appear in history. It will be found that increase of skill has not, of itself, insured any increase of human happiness or well-being. When men first learned to cultivate the soil, they used their knowledge to establish a cruel cult of human sacrifice. The men who first tamed the horse employed him to pillage and enslave peaceable populations. When, in the infancy of the industrial revolution, men discovered how to make cotton goods by machinery, the results were horrible: Jefferson's movement for the emancipation of slaves in America, which had been on the point of success, was killed dead; child labor in England was developed to a point of appalling cruelty; and ruthless imperialism in Africa was stimulated in the hope that black men could be induced to clothe themselves in cotton goods. In our own day a combination of scientific genius and technical skill has produced the atomic bomb, but having produced it we are all terrified, and do not know what to do with it. These instances, from widely different periods of history, show that something more than skill is required, something which may perhaps be called "wisdom." This is something that must be learned, if it can be learned, by means of other studies than those required for scientific technique. And it is something more needed now than ever before, because the rapid growth of technique has made ancient habits of thought and action more inadequate than in any earlier time.

"Philosophy" means "love of wisdom," and philosophy in this sense is what men must acquire if the new powers invented by technicians, and handed over by them to be wielded by ordinary men and women, are not to plunge mankind into an appalling cataclysm. But the philosophy that should be a part of general education is not the same thing as the philosophy of specialists. Not only in philosophy, but in all branches of academic study, there is a distinction between what has cultural value and what is only of professional interest. Historians may debate what happened to Sennacherib's unsuccessful expedition of 698 B.C., but those who are not historians need not know the difference between it and his successful expedition three years earlier. Professional Grecians may usefully discuss a disputed reading in a play of Aeschylus, but such matters are not for the man who wishes, in spite of a busy life, to acquire some knowledge of what the Greeks achieved. Similarly the men who devote their lives to philosophy must consider questions that the general educated public does right to ignore, such as the differences between the theory of universals in Aquinas and in Duns Scotus, or the characteristics that a language must have if it is to be able, without falling into nonsense, to say things about itself. Such questions belong to the technical aspects of philosophy, and their discussion cannot form part of its contribution to general culture.

Academic education should aim at giving, as a corrective of the specialization which increase of knowledge has made unavoidable, as much as time will permit of what has cultural value in such studies as history, literature, and philosophy. It should be made easy for a young man who knows no Greek to acquire through translations some understanding, however inadequate, of what the Greeks accomplished. Instead of studying the Anglo-Saxon kings over and over again at school, some attempt should be made to give a conspectus of world history, bringing the problems of our own day into relation with those of Egyptian priests, Babylonian kings, and Athenian reformers, as well as with all the hopes and despairs of the intervening centuries. But it is only of philosophy, treated from a similar point of view, that I wish to write.

Philosophy has had from its earliest days two different objects which were believed to be closely interrelated. On the one hand, it aimed at a theoretical understanding of the structure of the world; on the other hand, it tried to discover and inculcate the best possible way of life. From Heraclitus to Hegel, or even to Marx, it consistently kept both ends in view; it was neither purely theoretical nor purely practical, but sought a theory of the universe upon which to base a practical ethic.

Philosophy has thus been closely related to science on the one hand, and to religion on the other. Let us consider first the relation to science. Until the eighteenth century science was included in what was commonly called "philosophy," but since that time the word "philosophy" has been confined, on its theoretical side, to what is most speculative and general in the topics with which science deals. It is often said that philosophy is unprogressive, but this is largely a verbal matter: as soon as a way is found of arriving at definite knowledge on some ancient question, the new knowledge is counted as belonging to "science," and "philosophy" is deprived of the credit. In Greek times, and down to the time of Newton, planetary theory belonged to "philosophy," because it was uncertain and speculative, but Newton took the subject out of the realm of the free play of hypothesis, and made it one requiring a different type of skill from that which it had required when it was still open to fundamental doubts. Anaximander, in the sixth century B.C., had a theory of evolution, and maintained that men descended from fishes. This was philosophy because it was a speculation unsupported by detailed evidence, but Darwin's theory of evolution was science, because it was based on the succession of forms of life as found in fossils, and upon the distribution of animals and plants in many parts of the world. A man might say, with enough truth to justify a joke: "Science is what we know, and philosophy is what we don't know." But it should be added that philosophical speculation as to what we do not yet know has shown itself a valuable preliminary to exact scientific knowledge. The guesses of the Pythagoreans in astronomy, of Anaximander and Empedocles in biological evolution, and of Democritus as to the atomic constitution of matter, provided the men of science in later times with hypotheses which, but for the philosophers, might never have entered their heads. We may say that, on its theoretical side, philosophy consists, at least in part, in the framing of large general hypotheses which science is not yet in a position to test; but when it becomes possible to test the hypotheses they become, if verified, a part of science, and cease to count as "philosophy."

The utility of philosophy, on the theoretical side, is not confined to speculations which we may hope to see confirmed or confuted by science within a measurable time. Some men are so impressed by what science knows that they forget what it does not know; others are so much more interested in what it does not know than in what it does that they belittle its achievements. Those who think that science is everything become complacent and cocksure, and decry all interest in problems not having the circumscribed definiteness that is necessary for scientific treatment. In practical matters they tend to think that skill can take the place of wisdom, and that to kill each other by means of the latest technique is more "progressive," and therefore better, than to keep each other alive by old-fashioned methods. On the other hand, those who pooh-pooh science revert, as a rule, to some ancient and pernicious superstition, and refuse to admit the immense increase of human happiness which scientific technique, if wisely used, would make possible. Both these attitudes are to be deplored, and it is philosophy that shows the right attitude, by making clear at once the scope and the limitations of scientific knowledge.

Leaving aside, for the moment, all questions that have to do with ethics or with values, there are a number of purely theoretical questions, of perennial and passionate interest, which science is unable to answer, at any rate at present. Do we survive death in any sense, and if so, do we survive for a time or forever? Can mind dominate matter, or does matter completely dominate mind, or has each, perhaps, a certain limited independence? Has the universe a purpose? Or is it driven by blind necessity? Or is it a mere chaos and jumble, in which the natural laws that we think we find are only a fantasy generated by our own love of order? If there is a cosmic scheme, has life more importance in it than astronomy would lead us to suppose, or is our emphasis upon life mere parochialism and self-importance? I do not know the answer to these questions, and I do not believe that anybody else does, but I think human life would be impoverished if they were forgotten, or if definite answers were accepted without adequate evidence. To keep alive the interest in such questions, and to scrutinize suggested answers, is one of the functions of philosophy.

Those who have a passion for quick returns and for an exact balance sheet of effort and reward may feel impatient of a study which cannot, in the present state of our knowledge, arrive at certainties, and which encourages what may be thought the time-wasting occupation of inconclusive meditation on insoluble problems. To this view I cannot in any degree subscribe. Some kind of philosophy is a necessity to all but the most thoughtless, and in the absence of knowledge it is almost sure to be a silly philosophy. The result of this is that the human race becomes divided into rival groups of fanatics, each group firmly persuaded that its own brand of nonsense is sacred truth, while the other side's is damnable heresy. Arians and Catholics, Crusaders, and Moslems, Protestants and adherents of the Pope, Communists and Fascists, have filled large parts of the last 1,600 years with futile strife, when a little philosophy would have shown both sides in all these disputes that neither had any good reason to believe itself in the right. Dogmatism is an enemy to peace, and an insuperable barrier to democracy. In the present age, at least as much as in former times, it is the greatest of the mental obstacles to human happiness.

The demand for certainty is one which is natural to man, but is nevertheless an intellectual vice. If you take your children for a picnic on a doubtful day, they will demand a dogmatic answer as to whether it will be fine or wet, and be disappointed in you when you cannot be sure. The same sort of assurance is demanded, in later life, of those who undertake to lead populations into the Promised Land. "Liquidate the capitalists and the survivors will enjoy eternal bliss." "Exterminate the Jews and everyone will be virtuous." "Kill the Croats and let the Serbs reign." "Kill the Serbs and let the Croats reign." These are samples of the slogans that have won wide popular acceptance in our time. Even a modicum of philosophy would make it impossible to accept such bloodthirsty nonsense. But so long as men are not trained to withhold judgment in the absence of evidence, they will be led astray by cocksure prophets, and it is likely that their leaders will be either ignorant fanatics or dishonest charlatans. To endure uncertainty is difficult, but so are most of the other virtues. For the learning of every virtue there is an appropriate discipline, and for the learning of suspended judgment the best discipline is philosophy.

But if philosophy is to serve a positive purpose, it must not teach mere skepticism, for, while the dogmatist is harmful, the skeptic is useless. Dogmatism and skepticism are both, in a sense, absolute philosophies; one is certain of knowing, the other of not knowing. What philosophy should dissipate is *certainty*, whether of knowledge or of ignorance. Knowledge is not so precise a concept as is commonly thought. Instead of saying "I know this," we ought to say "I more or less know something more or less like this." It is true that this proviso is hardly necessary as regards the multiplication table, but knowledge in practical affairs has not the certainty or the precision of arithmetic. Suppose I say "democracy is a good thing": I must admit, first, that I am less sure of this than I am that two and two are four, and secondly, that "democracy" is a somewhat vague term which I cannot define precisely. We ought to say, therefore: "I am fairly certain that it is a good thing if a government has something of the characteristics that are common to the British and American Constitutions," or something of this sort. And one of the aims of education ought to be to make such a statement more effective from a platform than the usual type of political slogan.

For it is not enough to recognize that all our knowledge is, in a greater or less degree, uncertain and vague; it is necessary, at the same time, to learn to act upon the best hypothesis without dogmatically believing it. To revert to the picnic: even though you admit that it may rain, you start out if you think fine weather probable, but you allow for the opposite possibility by taking mackintoshes. If you were a dogmatist you would leave the mackintoshes at home. The same principles apply to more important issues. One may say broadly: all that passes for knowledge can be arranged in a hierarchy of degrees of certainty, with arithmetic and the facts of perception at the top. That two and two are four, and that I am sitting in my room writing, are statements as to which any serious doubt on my part would be pathological. I am nearly as certain that yesterday was a fine day, but not quite, because memory does sometimes play odd tricks. More distant memories are more doubtful, particularly if there is some strong emotional reason for remembering falsely, such, for instance, as made George IV remember being at the battle of Waterloo. Scientific laws may be very nearly certain, or only slightly probable, according to the state of the evidence.

When you act upon a hypothesis which you know to be uncertain, your action should be such as will not have *very* harmful results if your hypothesis is false. In the matter of the picnic, you may risk a wetting if all your party are robust, but not if one of them is so delicate as to run a risk of pneumonia. Or suppose you meet a Muggletonian, you will be justified in arguing with him, because not much harm will have been done if Mr. Muggleton was in fact as great a man as his disciples suppose, but you will not be justified in burning him at the stake, because the evil of being burned alive is more certain than any proposition of theology. Of course if the Muggletonians were so numerous and so fanatical that either you or they must be killed the question would grow more difficult, but the general principle remains, that an uncertain hypothesis cannot justify a certain evil unless an equal evil is equally certain on the opposite hypothesis.

Philosophy, we said, has both a theoretical and a practical aim. It is now time to consider the latter.

Among most of the philosophers of antiquity there was a close connection between a view of the universe and a doctrine as to the best way of life. Some of them founded fraternities which had a certain resemblance to the monastic orders of later times. Socrates and Plato were shocked by the sophists because they had no religious aims. If philosophy is to play a serious part in the lives of men who are not specialists, it must not cease to advocate some way of life. In doing this it is seeking to do something of what religion has done, but with certain differences. The greatest difference is that there is no appeal to authority, whether that of tradition or that of a sacred book. The second important difference is that a philosopher should not attempt to establish a church; Auguste Comte tried, but failed, as he deserved to do. The third is that more stress should be laid on the intellectual virtues than has been customary since the decay of Hellenic civilization.

There is one important difference between the ethical teachings of ancient philosophers and those appropriate to our own day. The ancient philosophers appealed to gentlemen of leisure, who could live as seemed good to them, and could even, if they chose, found an independent city having laws that embodied the master's doctrines. The immense majority of modern educated men have no such freedom; they have to earn their living within the existing framework of society, and they cannot make important changes in their own way of life unless they can first secure important changes in political and economic organization. The consequence is that a man's ethical convictions have to be expressed more in political advocacy, and less in his private behavior, than was the case in antiquity. And a conception of a good way of life has to be a social rather than an individual conception. Even among the ancients, it was so conceived by Plato in the *Republic*, but many of them had a more individualistic conception of the ends of life.

With this proviso, let us see what philosophy has to say on the subject of ethics.

To begin with the intellectual virtues: The pursuit of philosophy is founded on the belief that knowledge is good, even if what is known is painful. A man imbued with the philosophic spirit, whether a professional philosopher or not, will wish his beliefs to be as true as he can make them, and will, in equal measure, love to know, and hate to be in error. This principle has a wider scope than may be apparent at first sight. Our beliefs spring from a great variety of causes: what we were told in youth by parents and schoolteachers, what powerful organizations tell us in order to make us act as they wish, what either embodies or allays our fears, what ministers to our self-esteem, and so on. Any one of these causes may happen to lead us to true beliefs, but is more likely to lead us in the opposite direction. Intellectual sobriety, therefore, will lead us to scrutinize our beliefs closely, with a view to discovering which of them there is any reason to believe true. If we are wise, we shall apply solvent criticism especially to the beliefs that we find it most painful to doubt, and to those most likely to involve us in violent conflict with men who hold opposite but equally groundless beliefs. If this attitude could become common, the gain in diminishing the acerbity of disputes would be incalculable.

There is another intellectual virtue, which is that of generality or impartiality. I recommend the following exercise: When, in a sentence expressing political opinion, there are words that arouse powerful but different emotions in different readers, try replacing them by symbols, A, B, C, and so on, and forgetting the particular significance of the symbols. Suppose A is England, B is Germany and C is Russia. So long as you remember what the letters mean, most of the things you will believe will depend upon whether you are English, German or Russian, which is logically irrelevant. When, in elementary algebra, you do problems about A, B and C going up a mountain, you have no emotional interest in the gentlemen concerned, and you do your best to work out the solution with impersonal correctness. But if you thought that A was yourself, B your hated rival and C the schoolmaster who set the problem, your calculations would go askew, and you would be sure to find that A was first and C was last. In thinking about political problems this kind of emotional bias is bound to be present, and only care and practice can enable you to think as objectively as you do in the algebraic problem.

Thinking in abstract terms is of course not the only way to achieve ethical generality; it can be achieved as well, or perhaps even better, if you can feel generalized emotions. But to most people this is difficult. If you are hungry, you will make great exertions, if necessary, to get food; if your children are hungry, you may feel an even greater urgency. If a friend is starving, you will probably exert yourself to relieve his distress. But if you hear that some millions of Indians or Chinese are in danger of death from malnutrition, the problem is so vast and so distant that unless you have some official responsibility you probably soon forget all about it. Nevertheless, if you have the emotional capacity to feel distant evils acutely, you can achieve ethical generality through feeling. If you have not this rather rare gift, the habit of viewing practical problems abstractly as well as concretely is the best available substitute.

The interrelation of logical and emotional generality in ethics is an interesting subject. "Thou shalt love thy neighbor as thyself" inculcates emotional generality; "ethical statements should not contain proper names" inculcates logical generality. The two precepts *sound* very different, but when they are examined it will be found that they are scarcely distinguishable in practical import. Benevolent men will prefer the traditional form; logicians may prefer the other. I hardly know which class of men is the smaller. Either form of statement, if accepted by statesmen and tolerated by the populations whom they represent, would quickly lead to the millennium. Jews and Arabs would come together and say "Let us see how to get the greatest amount of good for both together, without inquiring too closely how it is distributed between us." Obviously each group would get far more of what makes for happiness of both than either can at present. The same would be true of Hindus and Moslems, Chinese Communists and adherents of Chiang Kai-shek, Italians and Yugoslavs, Russians and Western democrats. But alas! neither logic nor benevolence is to be expected on either side in any of these disputes.

It is not to be supposed that young men and women who are busy acquiring valuable specialized knowledge can spare a great deal of time for the study of philosophy, but even in the time that can easily be spared without injury to the learning of technical skills, philosophy can give certain things that will greatly increase the student's value as a human being and as a citizen. It can give a habit of exact and careful thought, not only in mathematics and science, but in questions of large practical import. It can give an impersonal breadth and scope to the conception of the ends of life. It can give to the individual a just measure of himself in relation to society, of man in the present to man in the past and in the future, and of the whole history of man in relation to the astronomical cosmos. By enlarging the objects of his thoughts it supplies an antidote to the anxieties and anguish of the present, and makes possible the nearest approach to serenity that is available to a sensitive mind in our tortured and uncertain world.

III

The Future of Mankind

BEFORE the end of the present century, unless something quite unforeseeable occurs, one of three possibilities will have been realized. These three are:

I. The end of human life, perhaps of all life on our planet.
II. A reversion to barbarism after a catastrophic diminution of the population of the globe.
III. A unification of the world under a single government, possessing a monopoly of all the major weapons of war.

l do not pretend to know which of these will happen, or even which is the most likely. What I do contend, without any hesitation, is that the kind of system to which we have been accustomed cannot possibly continue.

The first possibility, the extinction of the human race, is not to be expected in the next world war, unless that war is postponed for a longer time than now seems probable. But if the next world war is indecisive, or if the victors are unwise, and if organized states survive it, a period of feverish technical development may be expected to follow its conclusion. With vastly more powerful means of utilizing atomic energy than those now available, it is thought by many sober men of science that radio-active clouds, drifting round the world, may disintegrate living tissue everywhere. Although the last survivor may proclaim himself universal Emperor, his reign will be brief and his subjects will all be corpses. With his death the uneasy episode of life will end, and the peaceful rocks will revolve unchanged until the sun explodes.

Perhaps a disinterested spectator would consider this the most desirable consummation, in view of man's long record of folly and cruelty. But we, who are actors in the drama, who are entangled in the net of private affections and public hopes, can hardly take this attitude with any sincerity. True, I have heard men say that they would prefer the end of man to submission to the Soviet government, and doubtless in Russia there are those who would say the same about submission to Western capitalism. But this is rhetoric with a bogus air of heroism. Although it must be regarded as unimaginative humbug, it is dangerous, because it makes men less energetic in seeking ways of avoiding the catastrophe that they pretend not to dread.

The second possibility, that of a reversion to barbarism, would leave open the likelihood of a gradual return to civilization, as after the fall of Rome. The sudden transition will, if it occurs, be infinitely painful to those who experience it, and for some centuries afterwards life will be hard and drab. But at any rate there will still be a future for mankind, and the possibility of rational hope.

I think such an outcome of a really scientific world war is by no means improbable. Imagine each side in a position to destroy the chief cities and centers of industry of the enemy; imagine an almost complete obliteration of laboratories and libraries, accompanied by a heavy casualty rate among men of science; imagine famine due to radio-active spray, and pestilence caused by bacteriological warfare: would social cohesion survive such strains? Would not prophets tell the maddened populations that their ills were wholly due to science, and that the extermination of all educated men would bring the millennium? Extreme hopes are born of extreme misery, and in such a world hopes could only be irrational. I think the great states to which we are accustomed would break up, and the sparse survivors would revert to a primitive village economy.

The third possibility, that of the establishment of a single government for the whole world, might be realized in various ways: by the victory of the United States in the next world war, or by the victory of the U.S.S.R., or, theoretically, by agreement. Or—and I think this is the most hopeful of the issues that are in any degree probable—by an alliance of the nations that desire an international government, becoming, in the end, so strong that Russia would no longer dare to stand out. This might conceivably be achieved without another world war, but it would require courageous and imaginative statesmanship in a number of countries.

There are various arguments that are used against the project of a single government of the whole world. The commonest is that the project is utopian and impossible. Those who use this argument, like most of those who advocate a world government, are thinking of a world government brought about by agreement. I think it is plain that the mutual suspicions between Russia and the West make it futile to hope, in any near future, for any genuine agreement. Any pretended universal authority to which both sides can agree, as things stand, is bound to be a sham, like U.N.O. Consider the difficulties that have been encountered in the much more modest project of an international control over atomic energy, to which Russia will only consent if inspection is subject to the veto, and therefore a farce. I think we should admit that a world government will have to be imposed by force.

But—many people will say—why all this talk about a world government? Wars have occurred ever since men were organized into units larger than the family, but the human race has survived. Why should it not continue to survive even if wars go on occurring from time to time? Moreover, people like war, and will feel frustrated without it. And without war there will be no adequate opportunity for heroism or self-sacrifice.

This point of view—which is that of innumerable elderly gentlemen, including the rulers of Soviet Russia—fails to take account of modern technical possibilities. I think civilization could probably survive one more world war, provided it occurs fairly soon and does not last long. But if there is no slowing up in the rate of discovery and invention, and if great wars continue to recur, the destruction to be expected, even if it fails to exterminate the human race, is pretty certain to produce the kind of reversion to a primitive social system that I spoke of a moment ago. And this will entail such an enormous diminution of population, not only by war, but by subsequent starvation and disease, that the survivors are bound to be fierce and, at least for a considerable time, destitute of the qualities required for rebuilding civilization.

Nor is it reasonable to hope that, if nothing drastic is done, wars will nevertheless not occur. They always have occurred from time to time, and obviously will break out again sooner or later unless mankind adopt some system that makes them impossible. But the only such system is a single government with a monopoly of armed force.

If things are allowed to drift, it is obvious that the bickering between Russia and the Western democracies will continue until Russia has a considerable store of atomic bombs, and that when that time comes there will be an atomic war. In such a war, even if the worst consequences are avoided, Western Europe, including Great Britain, will be virtually exterminated. If America and the U.S.S.R. survive as organized states, they will presently fight again. If one side is victorious, it will rule the world, and a unitary government of mankind will have come into existence; if not, either mankind, or at least civilization, will perish. This is what must happen if nations and their rulers are lacking in constructive vision.

When I speak of "constructive vision," I do not mean merely the theoretical realization that a world government is desirable. More than half the American nation, according to the Gallup poll, hold this opinion. But most of its advocates think of it as something to be established by friendly negotiation, and shrink from any suggestion of the use of force. In this I think they are mistaken. I am sure that force, or the threat of force, will be necessary. I hope the threat of force may suffice, but, if not, actual force should be employed.

Assuming a monopoly of armed force established by the victory of one side in a war between the U.S. and the U.S.S.R., what sort of world will result?

In either case, it will be a world in which successful rebellion will be impossible. Although, of course, sporadic assassination will still be liable to occur, the concentration of all important weapons in the hands of the victors will make them irresistible, and there will therefore be secure peace. Even if the dominant nation is completely devoid of altruism, its leading inhabitants, at least, will achieve a very high level of material comfort, and will be freed from the tyranny of fear. They are likely, therefore, to become gradually more good-natured and less inclined to persecute. Like the Romans, they will, in the course of time, extend citizenship to the vanquished. There will then be a true world state, and it will be possible to forget that it will have owed its origin to conquest. Which of us, during the reign of Lloyd George, felt humiliated by the contrast with the days of Edward I?

A world empire of either the U.S. or the U.S.S.R. is therefore preferable to the results of a continuation of the present international anarchy.

There are, however, important reasons for preferring a vic-

tory of America. I am not contending that capitalism is better
than Communism; I think it not impossible that, if America
were Communist and Russia were capitalist, I should still be on
the side of America. My reason for siding with America is that
there is in that country more respect than in Russia for the
things that I value in a civilized way of life. The things I have
in mind are such as: freedom of thought, freedom of inquiry,
freedom of discussion, and humane feeling. What a victory of
Russia would mean is easily to be seen in Poland. There were
flourishing universities in Poland, containing men of great intellectual eminence. Some of these men, fortunately, escaped;
the rest disappeared. Education is now reduced to learning the
formula of Stalinist orthodoxy; it is only open (beyond the
elementary stage) to young people whose parents are politically irreproachable, and it does not aim at producing any
mental faculty except that of glib repetition of correct shib-
boleths and quick apprehension of the side that is winning official favor. From such an educational system nothing of intellectual value can result.

Meanwhile the middle class was annihilated by mass depor-
tations, first in 1940, and again after the expulsion of the Germans. Politicians of majority parties were liquidated, impris-
oned, or compelled to fly. Betraying friends to the police, or
perjury when they were brought to trial, are often the only
means of survival for those who have incurred governmental
suspicions.

I do not doubt that, if this régime continues for a generation,
it will succeed in its objects. Polish hostility to Russia will die
out, and be replaced by Communist orthodoxy. Science and
philosophy, art and literature, will become sycophantic adjuncts of government, jejune, narrow, and stupid. No individual will think, or even feel, for himself, but each will be contentedly a mere unit in the mass. A victory of Russia would,
in time, make such a mentality world-wide. No doubt the

complacency induced by success would ultimately lead to a relaxation of control, but the process would be slow, and the revival of respect for the individual would be doubtful. For such reasons I should view a Russian victory as an appalling disaster.

A victory by the United States would have far less drastic consequences. In the first place, it would not be a victory of the United States in isolation, but of an Alliance in which the other members would be able to insist upon retaining a large part of their traditional independence. One can hardly imagine the American army seizing the dons at Oxford and Cambridge and sending them to hard labor in Alaska. Nor do I think that they would accuse Mr. Attlee of plotting and compel him to fly to Moscow. Yet these are strict analogues to the things the Russians have done in Poland. After a victory of an Alliance led by the United States there would still be British culture, French culture, Italian culture, and (I hope) German culture; there would not, therefore, be the same dead uniformity as would result from Soviet domination.

There is another important difference, and that is that Moscow orthodoxy is much more all-pervasive than that of Washington. In America, if you are a geneticist, you may hold whatever view of Mendelism the evidence makes you regard as the most probable; in Russia, if you are a geneticist who disagrees with Lysenko, you are liable to disappear mysteriously. In America, you may write a book debunking Lincoln if you feel so disposed; in Russia, if you write a book debunking Lenin, it would not be published and you would be liquidated. If you are an American economist, you may hold, or not hold, that America is heading for a slump; in Russia, no economist dare question that an American slump is imminent. In America, if you are a professor of philosophy, you may be an idealist, a materialist, a pragmatist, a logical positivist, or whatever else may take your fancy; at congresses you can argue with men whose opinions differ from yours, and listeners can form a judgment as to who has the best of it. In Russia you must be a dialectical materialist, but at one time the element of materialism outweighs the element of dialectic, and at other times it is the other way round. If you fail to follow the developments of official metaphysics with sufficient nimbleness, it will be the worse for you. Stalin at all times knows the truth about metaphysics, but you must not suppose that the truth this year is the same as it was last year.

In such a world intellect must stagnate, and even technological progress must soon come to an end.

Liberty, of the sort that Communists despise, is important not only to intellectuals or to the more fortunate sections of society. Owing to its absence in Russia, the Soviet government has been able to establish a greater degree of economic inequality than exists in Great Britain, or even in America. An oligarchy which controls all the means of publicity can perpetrate injustices and cruelties which would be scarcely possible if they were widely known. Only democracy and free publicity can prevent the holders of power from establishing a servile state, with luxury for the few and overworked poverty for the many. This is what is being done by the Soviet government wherever it is in secure control. There are, of course, economic inequalities everywhere, but in a democratic régime they tend to diminish, whereas under an oligarchy they tend to increase. And wherever an oligarchy has power, economic inequalities threaten to become permanent owing to the modern impossibility of successful rebellion.

I come now to the question: what should be our policy, in view of the various dangers to which mankind is exposed? To summarize the above arguments: We have to guard against three dangers: (1) the extinction of the human race; (2) a reversion to barbarism; (3) the establishment of a universal slave state, involving misery for the vast majority, and the disappearance of all progress in knowledge and thought. Either the first or second of these disasters is almost certain unless great wars can soon be brought to an end. Great wars can only be brought to an end by the concentration of armed force under a single authority. Such a concentration cannot be brought about by agreement, because of the opposition of Soviet Russia, but it must be brought about somehow.

The first step—and it is one which is now not very difficult —is to persuade the United States and the British Commonwealth of the absolute necessity for a military unification of the world. The governments of the English-speaking nations should then offer to all other nations the option of entering into a firm Alliance, involving a pooling of military resources and mutual defense against aggression. In the case of hesitant nations, such as Italy, great inducements, economic and military, should be held out to produce their co-operation.

At a certain stage, when the Alliance had acquired sufficient strength, any Great Power still refusing to join should be threatened with outlawry, and, if recalcitrant, should be regarded as a public enemy. The resulting war, if it occurred fairly soon, would probably leave the economic and political structure of the United States intact, and would enable the victorious Alliance to establish a monopoly of armed force, and therefore to make peace secure. But perhaps, if the Alliance were sufficiently powerful, war would not be necessary, and the reluctant Powers would prefer to enter it as equals rather than, after a terrible war, submit to it as vanquished enemies. If this were to happen, the world might emerge from its present dangers without another great war. I do not see any hope of such a happy issue by any other method. But whether Russia would yield when threatened with war is a question as to which I do not venture an opinion.

I have been dealing mainly with the gloomy aspects of the present situation of mankind. It is necessary to do so, in order to persuade the world to adopt measures running counter to traditional habits of thought and ingrained prejudices. But beyond the difficulties and probable tragedies of the near future there is the possibility of immeasurable good, and of greater well-being than has ever before fallen to the lot of man. This is not merely a possibility, but, if the Western democracies are firm and prompt, a probability. From the break-up of the Roman Empire to the present day, states have almost continuously increased in size. There are now only two fully independent states, America and Russia. The next step in this long historical process should reduce the two to one, and thus put an end to the period of organized wars, which began in Egypt some 6,000 years ago. If war can be prevented without the establishment of a grinding tyranny, a weight will be lifted from the human spirit, deep collective fears will be exorcised, and as fear diminishes we may hope that cruelty also will grow less.

The uses to which men have put their increased control over natural forces are curious. In the nineteenth century they devoted themselves chiefly to increasing the numbers of *homo sapiens*, particularly of the white variety. In the twentieth century they have, so far, pursued the exactly opposite aim. Owing to the increased productivity of labor, it has become possible to devote a larger percentage of the population to war. If atomic energy were to make production easier, the only effect, as things are, would be to make wars worse, since fewer people would be needed for producing necessaries. Unless we can cope with the problem of abolishing war, there is no reason whatever to rejoice in labor-saving technique, but quite the reverse. On the other hand, if the danger of war were removed, scientific technique could at last be used to promote human happiness. There is no longer any technical reason for the persistence of poverty, even in such densely populated countries as India and China. If war no longer occupied men's thoughts and energies, we could, within a generation, put an end to all serious poverty throughout the world.

I have spoken of liberty as a good, but it is not an absolute good. We all recognize the need to restrain murderers, and it is even more important to restrain murderous states. Liberty must be limited by law, and its most valuable forms can only exist within a framework of law. What the world most needs is effective laws to control international relations. The first and most difficult step in the creation of such law is the establishment of adequate sanctions, and this is only possible through the creation of a single armed force in control of the whole world. But such an armed force, like a municipal police force, is not an end in itself; it is a means to the growth of a social system governed by law, where force is not the prerogative of private individuals or nations, but is exercised only by a neutral authority in accordance with rules laid down in advance. There is hope that law, rather than private force, may come to govern the relations of nations within the present century. If this hope is not realized we face utter disaster; if it is realized, the world will be far better than at any previous period in the history of man.

IV

Philosophy's Ulterior Motives

i

METAPHYSICS, according to F. H. Bradley, "is the finding of bad reasons for what we believe upon instinct." It is curious to find this pungent dictum at the beginning of a long book of earnest and even unctuous metaphysics, which, through much arduous argumentation, leads up to the final conclusion: "Outside of spirit there is not, and there cannot be, any reality, and, the more that anything is spiritual, so much the more is it veritably real." A rare moment of self-knowledge must have inspired the initial aphorism, which was made bearable to its author by its semi-humorous form; but throughout the rest of his labors he allowed himself to be claimed by "the instinct to find bad reasons." When he was serious he was sophistical, and a typical philosopher; when he jested, he had insight and uttered unphilosophical truth.

Philosophy has been defined as "an unusually obstinate attempt to think clearly"; I should define it rather as "an unusually ingenious attempt to think fallaciously." The philosopher's temperament is rare, because it has to combine two somewhat conflicting characteristics: on the one hand a strong desire to believe some general proposition about the universe or human life; on the other hand, inability to believe contentedly except on what appear to be intellectual grounds. The more profound the philosopher, the more intricate and subtle must his fallacies be in order to produce in him the desired state of intellectual acquiescence. That is why philosophy is obscure.

To the completely unintellectual, general doctrines are unimportant; to the man of science, they are hypotheses to be tested by experiment; while to the philosopher they are mental habits which must be justified somehow if he is to find life endurable. The typical philosopher finds certain beliefs emotionally indispensable, but intellectually difficult; he therefore goes through long chains of reasoning, in the course of which, sooner or later, a momentary lack of vigilance allows a fallacy to pass undetected. After the one false step, his mental agility quickly takes him far into the quagmire of falsehood.

Descartes, the father of modern philosophy, illustrates perfectly this peculiar mental temper. He would never—so he assures us—have been led to construct his philosophy if he had had only one teacher, for then he would have believed what he had been told; but, finding that his professors disagreed with each other, he was forced to conclude that no existing doctrine was certain. Having a passionate desire for certainty, he set to work to think out a new method of achieving it. As a first step, he determined to reject everything that he could bring himself to doubt. Everyday objects—his acquaintance, the streets, the sun and moon, and so on—might be illusions, for he saw similar things in dreams, and could not be certain that he was not always dreaming. The demonstrations in mathematics might be wrong, since mathematicians sometimes made mistakes. But he could not bring himself to doubt his own existence, since if he did not exist he could not doubt. Here at last, therefore, he had an indubitable premise for reconstruction of the intellectual edifices which his former skepticism had overthrown.

So far, so good. But from this moment his work loses all its critical acumen, and he accepts a host of scholastic maxims for which there is nothing to be said except the tradition of the schools. He believes that he exists, he says, because he sees this very clearly and very distinctly; he concludes, therefore, "that I may take as a general rule that the things which we conceive very clearly and very distinctly are all true." He then begins to conceive all sorts of things "very clearly and very distinctly," such as that an effect cannot have more perfection than its cause. Since he can form an idea of God—that is, of a being more perfect than himself—this idea must have had a cause other than himself, which can only be God; therefore God exists. Since God is good, He will not perpetually deceive Descartes; therefore the objects which Descartes sees when awake must really exist. And so on. All intellectual caution is thrown to the winds, and it might seem as if the initial skepticism had been merely rhetorical, though I do not believe that this would be psychologically true. Descartes's initial doubt was, I believe, as genuine as that of a man who has lost his way, but was equally intended to be replaced by certainty at the earliest possible moment.

In a man whose reasoning powers are good, fallacious arguments are evidence of bias. While Descartes is being skeptical, all that he says is acute and cogent, and even his first constructive step, the proof of his own existence, has much to be said in its favor. But everything that follows is loose and slip-shod and hasty, thereby displaying the distorting influence of desire. Something may be attributed to the need of appearing orthodox in order to escape persecution, but a more intimate cause must also have been at work. I do not suppose that he cared passionately about the reality of sensible objects, or even of God, but he did care about the truth of mathematics. And this, in his system, could only be established by first proving the existence and attributes of the Deity. His system, psychologically, was as follows: No God, no geometry; but geometry is delicious; therefore God exists.

Leibniz, who invented the phrase that "this is the best of all possible worlds," was a very different kind of man from Descartes. He was comfortable, not passionate; a professional, not an amateur. He made his living by writing the annals of the House of Hanover, and his reputation by bad philosophy. He also wrote good philosophy, but this he took care not to publish, as it would have cost him the pensions he received from various princes. One of his most important popular works, the *Théodicée*, was written for Queen Sophie Charlotte of Prussia (daughter of the Electress Sophia), as an antidote to the skepticism of Bayle's *Dictionary*. In this work he sets forth, in the authentic style of Voltaire's Dr. Pangloss, the grounds of optimism. He holds that there are many logically possible worlds, any one of which God could have created; that some of them contain no sin and no pain; and that in this actual world the number of the damned is incomparably greater than the number of the saved. But he thinks that worlds without evil contain so much less good than this world which God has chosen to create that they have a smaller excess of good over evil than it has. Leibniz and Queen Sophie Charlotte, who did not consider themselves likely to be among the damned, apparently found this type of optimism satisfying.

Beneath these superficialities there is a deeper problem, with which Leibniz struggled all his life. He wished to escape from the rigid necessity that characterized the determinist's world, without diminishing the empire of logic. The actual world, he thought, contains free will; moreover, God freely chose it in preference to any of the other possible worlds. But since they are less good than the actual world, the choice of one of them would have been incompatible with God's goodness; are we, then, to conclude that God is not *necessarily* good? Leibniz can hardly say this, for, like other philosophers, he believes it possible to find out important things, such as the nature of God, by merely sitting still and thinking; he shrinks, however, from the determinism which this view implies. He therefore takes refuge in obscurity and ambiguity. By great dexterity he avoids a sharp contradiction, but at the expense of the diffused muddle which pervades his whole system.

ii

A new method of apologetics was invented by the amiable Bishop Berkeley, who attacked the materialists of his day with the arguments which, in our time, have been revived by Sir James Jeans. His purpose was twofold: first, to prove that there can be no such thing as matter: secondly, to deduce from this negative proposition the necessary existence of God. On the first point, his contentions have never been answered; but I doubt whether he would have cared to advance them if he had not believed that they afforded support for theological orthodoxy.

When you think you see a tree, Berkeley points out that what you really know is not an external object, but a modification of yourself, a sensation, or, as he calls it, an "idea." This, which is all that you directly know, ceases if you shut your eyes. Whatever you can perceive is in your mind, not an external material object. Matter, therefore, is an unnecessary hypothesis. What is real about the tree is the perceptions of those who are supposed to "see" it; the rest is a piece of unnecessary metaphysics.

Up to this point, Berkeley's argumentation is able and largely valid. But now he suddenly changes his tone, and, after advancing a bold paradox, falls back upon the prejudices of the unphilosophical as the basis of his next thesis. He feels it preposterous to suppose that trees and houses, mountains and rivers, the sun and the moon and stars, only exist while we are looking at them, which is what his previous contentions suggest. There must, he thinks, be some permanence about physical objects, and some independence of human beings. This he secures by supposing that the tree is really an idea in the mind of God, and therefore continues to exist when no human being is looking at it. The consequences of his own paradox, if he had frankly accepted them, would have seemed to him dreadful; but by a sudden twist he rescues orthodoxy and some parts of common sense.

The same timidity in admitting the skeptical consequences of his argument has been shown by all his followers, except Hume; his most modern disciples have, in this respect, made no advance whatever upon him. None can bear to admit that *if* I know only "ideas" it is only *my* ideas that I know, and therefore I can have no reason to believe in the existence of anything except my own mental states. Those who have admitted the validity of this very simple argument have not been disciples of Berkeley, since they have found such a conclusion intolerable; they have therefore argued that it is not only "ideas" that we know.[1]

[1] The two sides of Berkeley's philosophy are illustrated by the following two limericks:

> There once was a man who said, "God
> Must think it exceedingly odd
> If he finds that this tree
> Continues to be
> When there's no one about in the Quad."
>   —RONALD KNOX

> Dear Sir,
>   Your astonishment's odd;
> *I* am always about in the Quad.
> And that's why the tree
> Will continue to be,
> Since observed by
>   Yours faithfully,
>   God.

Hume, the *enfant terrible* of philosophy, was peculiar in having no metaphysical ulterior motives. He was a historian and essayist as well as a philosopher, he had a comfortable temperament, and he perhaps derived as much pleasure from annoying the perpetrators of fallacies as he could have derived from inventing fallacies of his own. However, the main outcome of his activities was to stimulate two new sets of fallacies, one in England and the other in Germany. The German set are the more interesting.

The first German to take notice of Hume was Immanuel Kant, who had been content, up to the age of about forty-five, with the dogmatic tradition derived from Leibniz. Then, as he says himself, Hume "awakened him from his dogmatic slumbers." After meditating for twelve years, he produced his great work, the *Critique of Pure Reason;* seven years later, at the age of sixty-four, he produced the *Critique of Practical Reason,* in which he resumed his dogmatic slumbers after nearly twenty years of uncomfortable wakefulness. His fundamental desires were two: he wanted to be sure of an invariable routine, and he wanted to believe the moral maxims that he had learned in infancy. Hume was upsetting in both respects, for he maintained that we could not trust the law of causality, and he threw doubt on the future life, so that the good could not be sure of a reward in heaven. The first twelve years of Kant's meditations on Hume were devoted to the law of causality, and at the end he produced a remarkable solution. True, he said, we cannot know that there are causes in the real world, but then we cannot know anything about the real world. The world of appearances, which is the only one that we can experience, has all sorts of properties contributed by ourselves, just as a man who has a pair of green spectacles that he cannot take off is sure to see things green. The phenomena that we experience have causes, which are other phenomena; we need not worry as to whether there is causation in the reality behind the phenomena, since we cannot experience it. Kant went for a walk at exactly the same time every day, and his servant followed carrying the umbrella. The twelve years spent in producing the *Critique of Pure Reason* persuaded the old man that, if it came on to rain, the umbrella would prevent him from *feeling* wet, whatever Hume might say about the *real* raindrops.

This was comforting, but the comfort had been purchased at a great price. Space and time, in which phenomena take place, are unreal: Kant's psychical mechanism manufactured them. He did not know much about space, having never been more than ten miles from Königsberg; perhaps if he had traveled he would have doubted whether his subjective creativeness was equal to inventing the geography of all he saw. It was pleasant, however, to be sure of the truth of geometry, for, having manufactured space himself, he was quite sure that he had made it Euclidean, and he was sure of this without looking outside himself. In this way mathematics was got safely under the umbrella.

But although mathematics was safe, morality was still in danger. In the *Critique of Pure Reason* Kant taught that *pure* reason cannot prove the future life or the existence of God; it cannot therefore assure us that there is justice in the world. Moreover, there was a difficulty about free will. My actions, in so far as I can observe them, are phenomena, and therefore have causes. As to what my actions are in themselves, pure reason can tell me nothing, so that I do not know whether they are free or not. However, "pure" reason is not the only kind; there is another—not "impure," as might have been expected, but "practical." This starts from the premise that all the moral rules Kant was taught in childhood are true. (Such a premise, of course, needs a disguise; it is introduced to philosophical society under the name of the "categorical imperative.") It follows that the will is free, for it would be absurd to say "you *ought* to do so-and-so" unless you *can* do it. It follows also that there is a future life, since otherwise the good might not be adequately rewarded, nor the wicked adequately punished. It follows also that there must be a God to arrange these things. Hume may have routed "pure" reason, but the moral law has, in the end, restored the victory to the metaphysicians. So Kant died happy, and has been honored ever since; his doctrine has even been proclaimed the official philosophy of the Nazi state.

iii

Philosophers, for the most part, are constitutionally timid, and dislike the unexpected. Few of them would be genuinely happy as pirates or burglars. Accordingly they invent systems which make the future calculable, at least in its main outlines. The supreme practitioner in this art was Hegel. For him the course of logic and the course of history were broadly identical. Logic, for him, consisted of a series of self-correcting attempts to describe the world. If your first attempt is too simple, as it is sure to be, you will find that it contradicts itself; you will then try the opposite, or "antithesis," but this will also contradict itself. This leads you to a "synthesis," containing something of the original idea and something of its opposite, but more complex and less self-contradictory than either. This new idea, however, will also prove inadequate, and you will be driven, through its opposite, to a new synthesis. This process goes on until you reach the "Absolute Idea," in which there is no contradiction, and which, therefore, describes the real world.

But the real world, in Hegel as in Kant, is not the apparent world. The apparent world goes through developments which are the same as those that the logician goes through if he starts from Pure Being and travels on to the Absolute Idea. Pure

Being is exemplified by ancient China, of which Hegel knew only that it had existed; the Absolute Idea is exemplified by the Prussian state, which had given Hegel a professorship at Berlin. Why the world should go through this logical evolution is not clear; one is tempted to suppose that the Absolute Idea did not quite understand itself at first, and made mistakes when it tried to embody itself in events. But this, of course, was not what Hegel would have said.

Hegel's system satisfied the instincts of philosophers more fully than any of its predecessors. It was so obscure that no amateurs could hope to understand it. It was optimistic, since history is a progress in the unfolding of the Absolute Idea. It showed that the philosopher, sitting in his study considering abstract ideas, can know more about the real world than the statesman or the historian or the man of science. As to this, it must be admitted, there was an unfortunate incident. Hegel published his proof that there must be exactly seven planets just a week before the discovery of the eighth. The matter was hushed up, and a new, revised edition was hastily prepared; nevertheless, there were some who scoffed. But, in spite of this *contretemps*, Hegel's system was for a time triumphant in Germany. When it had been almost forgotten in its native country, it began to control the universities of Great Britain and America. Now, however, its adherents are a small and rapidly diminishing band. No subsequent great system has taken its place in the academic mind, and few now dare to say that the philosopher, by mere thinking without observation, can detect the errors of the man of science.

Outside the universities, however, one last great system has arisen from Hegel's ashes, and has kept alive in wide circles the happy faith in the power of thought which our professors have lost. This last survivor of an almost extinct species is the doctrine of Karl Marx. Marx took over from Hegel the belief in dialectic—that is to say, in logical development by thesis, antithesis, and synthesis, shown in the course of human history and not only in abstract thought. To Hegel, at the head of his profession and revered by his compatriots, it was possible to regard the Prussian state as the goal towards which all previous efforts had been tending; but to Marx, poor, ill, and in exile, it was obvious that the world is not yet perfect. One more turn of the dialectical wheel—that is to say, one more revolution—is necessary before the attainment of the millennium. There can be do doubt that this revolution will take place, for Marx, like Hegel, regards history as a logical process, so that its stages are as indubitable as arithmetic. Faith and hope thus find a place in Marxian doctrine.

Most of Marx's theory is independent of Hegel, but the Hegelian element is important, since it contributes the certainty of victory and the feeling of being on the side of irresistible cosmic forces. Emotionally, belief in Hegelian dialectic, when it exists in those whose present circumstances are unfortunate, is analogous to the Christian belief in the Second Coming; but its supposed logical basis gives it a hold on the head as well as the heart. Its hold on the head is endangered not so much by bourgeois prejudice as by the empirical scientific temper, which refuses to suppose that we can know as much about the universe as the metaphysicians supposed. Perhaps empirical sobriety is so difficult that men will never preserve it except when they are happy. If so, the various irrational faiths of our time are a natural outcome of our self-imposed misfortunes, and a new era of metaphysics may be inspired by new disasters.

iv

Philosophy is a stage in intellectual development, and is not compatible with mental maturity. In order that it may flourish, traditional doctrines must still be believed, but not so unquestioningly that arguments in support of them are never sought; there must also be a belief that important truths can be discovered by merely thinking, without the aid of observation. This belief is true in pure mathematics, which has inspired many of the great philosophers. It is true in mathematics because that study is essentially verbal; it is not true elsewhere, because thought alone cannot establish any non-verbal fact. Savages and barbarians believe in a magical connection between persons and their names, which makes it dangerous to let an enemy know what they are called. The distinction between words and what they designate is one which it is difficult always to remember; metaphysicians, like savages, are apt to imagine a magical connection between words and things, or at any rate between syntax and world structure. Sentences have subjects and predicates, therefore the world consists of substances with attributes. Until very recently this argument was accepted as valid by almost all philosophers; or rather, it controlled their opinions almost without their own knowledge.

In addition to confusion between language and what it means, there is another source of the belief that the philosopher can find out facts by mere thinking; this is the conviction that the world must be ethically satisfying. Dr. Pangloss in his study can ascertain what sort of universe would, to his way of thinking, be the best possible; he can also convince himself, so long as he stays in his study, that the universe means to satisfy his ethical demands. Bernard Bosanquet, until his death one of the recognized leaders of British philosophy, maintained in his *Logic*, ostensibly on logical grounds, that "it would be hard to believe, for example, in the likelihood of a catastrophe which should overwhelm a progressive civilization like that of modern Europe and its colonies." Capacity to believe that the "laws of thought" have comforting political consequences is a mark of the philosophic bias. Philosophy, as opposed to science, springs from a kind of self-assertion: a belief that our purposes have an important relation to the purposes of the universe, and that, in the long run, the course of events is bound to be, on the whole, such as we should wish. Science abandoned this kind of optimism, but is being led towards another: that we, by our intelligence, can make the world such as to satisfy a large proportion of our desires. This is a practical, as opposed to a metaphysical, optimism. I hope it will not seem to future generations as foolish as that of Dr. Pangloss.

V

The Superior Virtue of the

Oppressed

O NE of the persistent delusions of mankind is that some sections of the human race are morally better or worse than others. This belief has many different forms, none of which has any rational basis. It is natural to think well of ourselves, and thence, if our mental processes are simple, of our sex, our class, our nation, and our age. But among writers, especially moralists, a less direct expression of self-esteem is common. They tend to think ill of their neighbors and acquaintances, and therefore to think well of the sections of mankind to which they themselves do not belong. Lao-tse admired the "pure men of old," who lived before the advent of Confucian sophistication. Tacitus and Madame de Staël admired the Germans because they had no emperor. Locke thought well of the "intelligent American" because he was not led astray by Cartesian sophistries.

A rather curious form of this admiration for groups to which the admirer does not belong is the belief in the superior virtue of the oppressed: subject nations, the poor, women, and children. The eighteenth century, while conquering America

from the Indians, reducing the peasantry to the condition of
pauper laborers, and introducing the cruelties of early industrialism, loved to sentimentalize about the "noble savage" and
the "simple annals of the poor." Virtue, it was said, was not to
be found in courts: but court ladies could *almost* secure it by
masquerading as shepherdesses. And as for the male sex:

> Happy the man whose wish and care
> A few paternal acres bound.

Nevertheless, for himself Pope preferred London and his villa
at Twickenham.

At the French Revolution the superior virtue of the poor
became a party question, and has remained so ever since. To
reactionaries they became the "rabble" or the "mob." The rich
discovered, with surprise, that some people were so poor as
not to own even "a few paternal acres." Liberals, however,
still continued to idealize the rural poor, while intellectual
Socialists and Communists did the same for the urban proletariat—a fashion to which, since it only became important in
the twentieth century, I shall return later.

Nationalism introduced, in the nineteenth century, a substitute for the noble savage—the patriot of an oppressed nation. The Greeks until they had achieved liberation from the
Turks, the Hungarians until the *Ausgleich* of 1867, the Italians
until 1870, and the Poles until after the 1914–18 war were regarded romantically as gifted poetic races, too idealistic to
succeed in this wicked world. The Irish were regarded by the
English as possessed of a special charm and mystical insight
until 1921, when it was found that the expense of continuing
to oppress them would be prohibitive. One by one these various nations rose to independence, and were found to be just
like everybody else; but the experience of those already liber-
ated did nothing to destroy the illusion as regards those who
were still struggling. English old ladies still sentimentalize

about the "wisdom of the East" and American intellectuals about the "earth consciousness" of the Negro.

Women, being the objects of the strongest emotions, have been viewed even more irrationally than the poor or the subject nations. I am thinking not of what poets have to say but of the sober opinions of men who imagine themselves rational. The church had two opposite attitudes: on the one hand, woman was the Temptress, who led monks and others into sin; on the other hand, she was capable of saintliness to an almost greater degree than man. Theologically, the two types were represented by Eve and the Virgin. In the nineteenth century the temptress fell into the background; there were, of course, "bad" women, but Victorian worthies, unlike St. Augustine and his successors, would not admit that such sinners could tempt them, and did not like to acknowledge their existence. A kind of combination of the Madonna and the lady of chivalry was created as the ideal of the ordinary married woman. She was delicate and dainty, she had a bloom which would be rubbed off by contact with the rough world, she had ideals which might be dimmed by contact with wickedness; like the Celts and the Slavs and the noble savage, but to an even greater degree, she enjoyed a spiritual nature, which made her the superior of man but unfitted her for business or politics or the control of her own fortune. This point of view is still not entirely extinct. Not long ago, in reply to a speech I had made in favor of equal pay for equal work, an English schoolmaster sent me a pamphlet published by a schoolmasters' association, setting forth the opposite opinion, which it supports with curious arguments. It says of woman: "We gladly place her first as a spiritual force; we acknowledge and reverence her as the 'angelic part of humanity'; we give her superiority in all the graces and refinements we are capable of as human beings; we wish her to retain all her winsome womanly ways." "This appeal"—that women should be content with lower rates of pay—"goes forth from us to them," so we are assured, "in no selfish spirit, but out of respect and devotion to our mothers, wives, sisters, and daughters. . . . Our purpose is a sacred one, a real spiritual crusade."

Fifty or sixty years ago such language would have roused no comment except on the part of a handful of feminists; now, since women have acquired the vote, it has come to seem an anachronism. The belief in their "spiritual" superiority was part and parcel of the determination to keep them inferior economically and politically. When men were worsted in this battle, they had to respect women, and therefore gave up offering them "reverence" as a consolation for inferiority.

A somewhat similar development has taken place in the adult view of children. Children, like women, were theologically wicked, especially among evangelicals. They were limbs of Satan, they were unregenerate; as Dr. Watts so admirably put it:

> One stroke of His almighty rod
> Can send young sinners quick to Hell.

It was necessary that they should be "saved." At Wesley's school "a general conversion was once effected, . . . one poor boy only excepted, who unfortunately resisted the influence of the Holy Spirit, for which he was severely flogged. . . ." But during the nineteenth century, when parental authority, like that of kings and priests and husbands, felt itself threatened, subtler methods of quelling insubordination came into vogue. Children were "innocent"; like good women they had a "bloom"; they must be protected from knowledge of evil lest their bloom should be lost. Moreover, they had a special kind of wisdom. Wordsworth made this view popular among English-speaking people. He first made it fashionable to credit children with

> High instincts before which our mortal nature
> Did tremble like a guilty thing surprised.

No one in the eighteenth century would have said to his little daughter, unless she were dead:

> Thou liest in Abraham's bosom all the year
> And worships't at the temple's inner shrine.

But in the nineteenth century this view became quite common; and respectable members of the Episcopal church—or even of the Catholic church—shamelessly ignored Original Sin to dally with the fashionable heresy that

> . . . trailing clouds of glory do we come
> From God who is our home:
> Heaven lies about us in our infancy.

This led to the usual development. It began to seem hardly right to spank a creature that was lying in Abraham's bosom, or to use the rod rather than "high instincts" to make it "tremble like a guilty thing surprised." And so parents and school-masters found that the pleasures they had derived from inflicting chastisement were being curtailed and a theory of education grew up which made it necessary to consider the child's welfare, and not only the adult's convenience and sense of power.

The only consolation the adults could allow themselves was the invention of a new child psychology. Children, after being limbs of Satan in traditional theology and mystically illuminated angels in the minds of educational reformers, have reverted to being little devils—not theological demons inspired by the Evil One, but scientific Freudian abominations inspired by the Unconscious. They are, it must be said, far more wicked than they were in the diatribes of the monks; they display, in modern textbooks, an ingenuity and persistence in sinful imaginings to which in the past there was nothing comparable except St. Anthony. Is all this the objective truth at last? Or is it merely an adult imaginative compensation for being no longer allowed to wallop the little pests? Let the Freudians answer, each for the others.

As appears from the various instances that we have considered, the stage in which superior virtue is attributed to the oppressed is transient and unstable. It begins only when the oppressors come to have a bad conscience, and this only happens when their power is no longer secure. The idealizing of the victim is useful for a time: if virtue is the greatest of goods, and if subjection makes people virtuous, it is kind to refuse them power, since it would destroy their virtue. If it is difficult for a rich man to enter the kingdom of heaven, it is a noble act on his part to keep his wealth and so imperil his eternal bliss for the benefit of his poorer brethren. It was a fine self-sacrifice on the part of men to relieve women of the dirty work of politics. And so on. But sooner or later the oppressed class will argue that its superior virtue is a reason in favor of its having power, and the oppressors will find their own weapons turned against them. When at last power has been equalized, it becomes apparent to everybody that all the talk about superior virtue was nonsense, and that it was quite unnecessary as a basis for the claim to equality.

In regard to the Italians, the Hungarians, women, and children, we have run through the whole cycle. But we are still in the middle of it in the case which is of the most importance at the present time—namely, that of the proletariat. Admiration of the proletariat is very modern. The eighteenth century, when it praised "the poor," thought always of the rural poor. Jefferson's democracy stopped short at the urban mob; he wished America to remain a country of agriculturists. Admiration of the proletariat, like that of dams, power stations, and airplanes, is part of the ideology of the machine age. Considered in human terms, it has as little in its favor as belief in Celtic magic, the Slav soul, women's intuition, and children's innocence. If it were indeed the case that bad nourishment, little education, lack of air and sunshine, unhealthy housing conditions, and overwork produce better people than are produced by good nourishment, open air, adequate education and housing, and a reasonable amount of leisure, the whole case for economic reconstruction would collapse, and we could rejoice that such a large percentage of the population enjoys the conditions that make for virtue. But obvious as this argument is, many Socialist and Communist intellectuals consider it *de rigueur* to pretend to find the proletariat more amiable than other people, while professing a desire to abolish the conditions which, according to them, alone produce good human beings. Children were idealized by Wordsworth and un-idealized by Freud. Marx was the Wordsworth of the proletariat; its Freud is still to come.

VI

On Being Modern-minded

OUR age is the most parochial since Homer. I speak not of any geographical parish: the inhabitants of Mudcombe-in-the-Meer are more aware than at any former time of what is being done and thought at Praha, at Gorki, or at Peiping. It is in the chronological sense that we are parochial: as the new names conceal the historic cities of Prague, Nijni-Novgorod, and Pekin, so new catchwords hide from us the thoughts and feelings of our ancestors, even when they differed little from our own. We imagine ourselves at the apex of intelligence, and cannot believe that the quaint clothes and cumbrous phrases of former times can have invested people and thoughts that are still worthy of our attention. If *Hamlet* is to be interesting to a really modern reader, it must first be translated into the language of Marx or of Freud, or, better still, into a jargon inconsistently compounded of both. I read some years ago a contemptuous review of a book by Santayana, mentioning an essay on Hamlet "dated, in every sense, 1908"—as if what has been discovered since then made any earlier appreciation of Shakespeare irrelevant and comparatively superficial. It did not occur to the reviewer that his review was "dated, in every sense, 1936." Or perhaps this thought did occur to him, and filled him with satisfaction. He was writing for the moment, not for all time; next year he will have adopted the new fashion in opinions, whatever it may be, and he no doubt hopes to remain up to date as long as he continues to write. Any other ideal for a writer would seem absurd and old-fashioned to the modern-minded man.

The desire to be contemporary is of course new only in degree; it has existed to some extent in all previous periods that believed themselves to be progressive. The Renaissance had a contempt for the Gothic centuries that had preceded it; the seventeenth and eighteenth centuries covered priceless mosaics with whitewash; the Romantic movement despised the age of the heroic couplet. Eighty years ago Lecky reproached my mother for being led by intellectual fashion to oppose fox-hunting: "I am sure," he wrote, "you are not really at all sentimental about foxes or at all shocked at the prettiest of the assertions of women's rights, riding across country. But you always look upon politics and intellect as a fierce race and are so dreadfully afraid of not being sufficiently advanced or intellectual." But in none of these former times was the contempt for the past nearly as complete as it is now. From the Renaissance to the end of the eighteenth century men admired Roman antiquity; the Romantic movement revived the Middle Ages; my mother, for all her belief in nineteenth-century progress, constantly read Shakespeare and Milton. It is only since the 1914–18 war that it has been fashionable to ignore the past *en bloc*.

The belief that fashion alone should dominate opinion has great advantages. It makes thought unnecessary and puts the highest intelligence within the reach of everyone. It is not difficult to learn the correct use of such words as "complex," "sadism," "Oedipus," "bourgeois," "deviation," "left"; and nothing more is needed to make a brilliant writer or talker. Some, at least, of such words represented much thought on the part of their inventors; like paper money they were originally convertible into gold. But they have become for most people inconvertible, and in depreciating have increased nominal wealth in ideas. And so we are enabled to despise the paltry intellectual fortunes of former times.

The modern-minded man, although he believes profoundly in the wisdom of his period, must be presumed to be very modest about his personal powers. His highest hope is to think first what is about to be thought, to say what is about to be said, and to feel what is about to be felt; he has no wish to think better thoughts than his neighbors, to say things showing more insight, or to have emotions which are not those of some fashionable group, but only to be slightly ahead of others in point of time. Quite deliberately he suppresses what is individual in himself for the sake of the admiration of the herd. A mentally solitary life, such as that of Copernicus, or Spinoza, or Milton after the Restoration, seems pointless according to modern standards. Copernicus should have delayed his advocacy of the Copernican system until it could be made fashionable; Spinoza should have been either a good Jew or a good Christian; Milton should have moved with the times, like Cromwell's widow, who asked Charles II for a pension on the ground that she did not agree with her husband's politics. Why should an individual set himself up as an independent judge? Is it not clear that wisdom resides in the blood of the Nordic race or, alternatively, in the proletariat? And in any case what is the use of an eccentric opinion, which never can hope to conquer the great agencies of publicity?

The money rewards and widespread though ephemeral fame which those agencies have made possible places temptations in the way of able men which are difficult to resist. To be pointed out, admired, mentioned constantly in the press, and offered easy ways of earning much money is highly agreeable; and when all this is open to a man, he finds it difficult to go on doing the work that he himself thinks best and is inclined to subordinate his judgment to the general opinion.

Various other factors contribute to this result. One of these is the rapidity of progress which has made it difficult to do work which will not soon be superseded. Newton lasted till Einstein; Einstein is already regarded by many as antiquated. Hardly any man of science, nowadays, sits down to write a great work, because he knows that, while he is writing it, others will discover new things that will make it obsolete before it appears. The emotional tone of the world changes with equal rapidity, as wars, depressions, and revolutions chase each other across the stage. And public events impinge upon private lives more forcibly than in former days. Spinoza, in spite of his heretical opinions, could continue to sell spectacles and meditate, even when his country was invaded by foreign enemies; if he had lived now, he would in all likelihood have been conscripted or put in prison. For these reasons a greater energy of personal conviction is required to lead a man to stand out against the current of his time than would have been necessary in any previous period since the Renaissance.

The change has, however, a deeper cause. In former days men wished to serve God. When Milton wanted to exercise "that one talent which is death to hide," he felt that his soul was "bent to serve therewith my Maker." Every religiously minded artist was convinced that God's aesthetic judgments coincided with his own; he had therefore a reason, independent of popular applause, for doing what he considered his best, even if his style was out of fashion. The man of science in pursuing truth, even if he came into conflict with current superstition, was still setting forth the wonders of Creation and bringing men's imperfect beliefs more nearly into harmony with God's perfect knowledge. Every serious worker, whether artist, philosopher, or astronomer, believed that in following his own convictions he was serving God's purposes. When with the progress of enlightenment this belief began to grow dim, there still remained the True, the Good, and the Beautiful. Non-human standards were still laid up in heaven, even if heaven had no topographical existence.

Throughout the nineteenth century the True, the Good, and the Beautiful preserved their precarious existence in the minds of earnest atheists. But their very earnestness was their undoing, since it made it impossible for them to stop at a half-way house. Pragmatists explained that Truth is what it pays to believe. Historians of morals reduced the Good to a matter of tribal custom. Beauty was abolished by the artists in a revolt against the sugary insipidities of a philistine epoch and in a mood of fury in which satisfaction is to be derived only from what hurts. And so the world was swept clear not only of God as a person but of God's essence as an ideal to which man owed an ideal allegiance; while the individual, as a result of a crude and uncritical interpretation of sound doctrines, was left without any inner defense against social pressure.

All movements go too far, and this is certainly true of the movement toward subjectivity, which began with Luther and Descartes as an assertion of the individual and has culminated by an inherent logic in his complete subjection. The subjectivity of truth is a hasty doctrine not validly deducible from the premises which have been thought to imply it; and the habits of centuries have made many things seem dependent upon theological belief which in fact are not so. Men lived with one kind of illusion, and when they lost it they fell into another. But it is not by old error that new error can be combated. Detachment and objectivity, both in thought and in feeling, have been historically but not logically associated with certain traditional beliefs; to preserve them without these beliefs is both possible and important. A certain degree of isolation both in space and time is essential to generate the independence required for the most important work; there must be something which is felt to be of more importance than the admiration of the contemporary crowd. We are suffering not from the decay of theological beliefs but from the loss of solitude.

VII

An Outline of Intellectual

Rubbish

MAN is a rational animal—so at least I have been told. Throughout a long life, I have looked diligently for evidence in favor of this statement, but so far I have not had the good fortune to come across it, though I have searched in many countries spread over three continents. On the contrary, I have seen the world plunging continually further into madness. I have seen great nations, formerly leaders of civilization, led astray by preachers of bombastic nonsense. I have seen cruelty, persecution, and superstition increasing by leaps and bounds, until we have almost reached the point where praise of rationality is held to mark a man as an old fogey regrettably surviving from a bygone age. All this is depressing, but gloom is a useless emotion. In order to escape from it, I have been driven to study the past with more attention than I had formerly given to it, and have found, as Erasmus found, that folly is perennial and yet the human race has survived. The follies of our own times are easier to bear when they are seen against the background of past follies. In what follows I shall mix the sillinesses of our day with those of former centuries. Perhaps the result may help in seeing our own times in perspective, and as not much worse than other ages that our ancestors lived through without ultimate disaster.

Aristotle, so far as I know, was the first man to proclaim explicitly that man is a rational animal. His reason for this view was one which does not now seem very impressive; it was that some people can do sums. He thought that there are three kinds of soul: the vegetable soul, possessed by all living things, both plants and animals, and concerned only with nourishment and growth; the animal soul, concerned with locomotion, and shared by man with the lower animals; and finally the rational soul, or intellect, which is the Divine mind, but in which men participate to a greater or less degree in proportion to their wisdom. It is in virtue of the intellect that man is a rational animal. The intellect is shown in various ways, but most emphatically by mastery of arithmetic. The Greek system of numerals was very bad, so that the multiplication table was quite difficult, and complicated calculations could only be made by very clever people. Nowadays, however, calculating machines do sums better than even the cleverest people, yet no one contends that these useful instruments are immortal, or work by divine inspiration. As arithmetic has grown easier, it has come to be less respected. The consequence is that, though many philosophers continue to tell us what fine fellows we are, it is no longer on account of our arithmetical skill that they praise us.

Since the fashion of the age no longer allows us to point to calculating boys as evidence that man is rational and the soul, at least in part, immortal, let us look elsewhere. Where shall we look first? Shall we look among eminent statesmen, who have so triumphantly guided the world into its present condition? Or shall we choose the men of letters? Or the philoso-

phers? All these have their claims, but I think we should begin
with those whom all right-thinking people acknowledge to be
the wisest as well as the best of men, namely the clergy. If *they*
fail to be rational, what hope is there for us lesser mortals?
And alas—though I say it with all due respect—there have
been times when their wisdom has not been very obvious, and,
strange to say, these were especially the times when the power
of the clergy was greatest.

The Ages of Faith, which are praised by our neo-scholastics,
were the time when the clergy had things all their own way.
Daily life was full of miracles wrought by saints and wizardry
perpetrated by devils and necromancers. Many thousands of
witches were burned at the stake. Men's sins were punished by
pestilence and famine, by earthquake, flood, and fire. And yet,
strange to say, they were even more sinful than they are nowadays. Very little was known scientifically about the world.
A few learned men remembered Greek proofs that the earth
is round, but most people made fun of the notion that there
are antipodes. To suppose that there are human beings at the
antipodes was heresy. It was generally held (though modern
Catholics take a milder view) that the immense majority of
mankind are damned. Dangers were held to lurk at every turn.
Devils would settle on the food that monks were about to eat,
and would take possession of the bodies of incautious feeders
who omitted to make the sign of the Cross before each mouth-
ful. Old-fashioned people still say "bless you" when one
sneezes, but they have forgotten the reason for the custom.
The reason was that people were thought to sneeze out their
souls, and before their souls could get back lurking demons
were apt to enter the un-souled body; but if anyone said
"God bless you," the demons were frightened off.

Throughout the last 400 years, during which the growth
of science has gradually shown men how to acquire knowledge

of the ways of nature and mastery over natural forces, the clergy have fought a losing battle against science, in astronomy and geology, in anatomy and physiology, in biology and psychology and sociology. Ousted from one position, they have taken up another. After being worsted in astronomy, they did their best to prevent the rise of geology; they fought against Darwin in biology, and at the present time they fight against scientific theories of psychology and education. At each stage, they try to make the public forget their earlier obscurantism, in order that their present obscurantism may not be recognized for what it is. Let us note a few instances of irrationality among the clergy since the rise of science, and then inquire whether the rest of mankind are any better.

When Benjamin Franklin invented the lightning-rod, the clergy, both in England and America, with the enthusiastic support of George III, condemned it as an impious attempt to defeat the will of God. For, as all right-thinking people were aware, lightning is sent by God to punish impiety or some other grave sin—the virtuous are never struck by lightning. Therefore if God wants to strike anyone, Benjamin Franklin ought not to defeat His design; indeed, to do so is helping criminals to escape. But God was equal to the occasion, if we are to believe the eminent Dr. Price, one of the leading divines of Boston. Lightning having been rendered ineffectual by the "iron points invented by the sagacious Dr. Franklin," Massachusetts was shaken by earthquakes, which Dr. Price perceived to be due to God's wrath at the "iron points." In a sermon on the subject he said, "In Boston are more erected than elsewhere in New England, and Boston seems to be more dreadfully shaken. Oh! there is no getting out of the mighty hand of God." Apparently, however, Providence gave up all hope of curing Boston of its wickedness, for, though lightning-rods became more and more common, earthquakes in Massachusetts have remained rare. Nevertheless, Dr. Price's point of view, or something very like it, was still held by one of the most influential men of recent times. When, at one time, there were several bad earthquakes in India, Mahatma Gandhi solemnly warned his compatriots that these disasters had been sent as a punishment for their sins.

Even in my own native island this point of view still exists. During the 1914–18 war, the British government did much to stimulate the production of food at home. In 1916, when things were not going well, a Scottish clergyman wrote to the newspapers to say that military failure was due to the fact that, with government sanction, potatoes had been planted on the Sabbath. However, disaster was averted, owing to the fact that the Germans disobeyed *all* the Ten Commandments, and not only one of them.

Sometimes, if pious men are to be believed, God's mercies are curiously selective. Toplady, the author of *Rock of Ages*, moved from one vicarage to another; a week after the move, the vicarage he had formerly occupied burned down, with great loss to the new vicar. Thereupon Toplady thanked God; but what the new vicar did is not known. Borrow, in his *Bible in Spain*, records how without mishap he crossed a mountain pass infested by bandits. The next party to cross, however, were set upon, robbed, and some of them murdered; when Borrow heard of this, he, like Toplady, thanked God.

Although we are taught the Copernican astronomy in our textbooks, it has not yet penetrated to our religion or our morals, and has not even succeeded in destroying belief in astrology. People still think that the Divine Plan has special reference to human beings, and that a special Providence not only looks after the good, but also punishes the wicked. I am sometimes shocked by the blasphemies of those who think themselves pious—for instance, the nuns who never take a bath without wearing a bathrobe all the time. When asked why, since no man can see them, they reply: "Oh, but you forget the good

God." Apparently they conceive of the Deity as a Peeping Tom, whose omnipotence enables Him to see through bathroom walls, but who is foiled by bathrobes. This view strikes me as curious.

The whole conception of "Sin" is one which I find very puzzling, doubtless owing to my sinful nature. If "Sin" consisted in causing needless suffering, I could understand; but on the contrary, sin often consists in avoiding needless suffering. Some years ago, in the English House of Lords, a bill was introduced to legalize euthanasia in cases of painful and incurable disease. The patient's consent was to be necessary, as well as several medical certificates. To me, in my simplicity, it would seem natural to require the patient's consent, but the late Archbishop of Canterbury, the English official expert on Sin, explained the erroneousness of such a view. The patient's consent turns euthanasia into suicide, and suicide is sin. Their Lordships listened to the voice of authority, and rejected the bill. Consequently, to please the Archbishop—and his God, if he reports truly—victims of cancer still have to endure months of wholly useless agony, unless their doctors or nurses are sufficiently humane to risk a charge of murder. I find difficulty in the conception of a God who gets pleasure from contemplating such tortures; and if there were a God capable of such wanton cruelty, I should certainly not think Him worthy of worship. But that only proves how sunk I am in moral depravity.

I am equally puzzled by the things that are sin and by the things that are not. When the Society for the Prevention of Cruelty to Animals asked the Pope for his support, he refused it, on the ground that human beings owe no duty to the lower animals, and that ill-treating animals is not sinful. This is because animals have no souls. On the other hand, it is wicked to marry your deceased wife's sister—so at least the church teaches—however much you and she may wish to marry. This is not because of any unhappiness that might result, but because of certain texts in the Bible.

The resurrection of the body, which is an article of the Apostle's Creed, is a dogma which has various curious consequences. There was an author not very many years ago, who had an ingenious method of calculating the date of the end of the world. He argued that there must be enough of the necessary ingredients of a human body to provide everybody with the requisites at the Last Day. By carefully calculating the available raw material, he decided that it would all have been used up by a certain date. When that date comes, the world must end, since otherwise the resurrection of the body would become impossible. Unfortunately, I have forgotten what the date was, but I believe it is not very distant.

St. Thomas Aquinas, the official philosopher of the Catholic church, discussed lengthily and seriously a very grave problem, which, I fear, modern theologians unduly neglect. He imagines a cannibal who has never eaten anything but human flesh, and whose father and mother before him had like propensities. Every particle of his body belongs rightfully to someone else. We cannot suppose that those who have been eaten by cannibals are to go short through all eternity. But, if not, what is left for the cannibal? How is he to be properly roasted in hell, if all his body is restored to its original owners? This is a puzzling question, as the Saint rightly perceives.

In this connection the orthodox have a curious objection to cremation, which seems to show an insufficient realization of God's omnipotence. It is thought that a body which has been burned will be more difficult for Him to collect together again than one which has been put underground and transformed into worms. No doubt collecting the particles from the air and undoing the chemical work of combustion would be somewhat laborious, but it is surely blasphemous to suppose such a work impossible for the Deity. I conclude that the objection to cremation implies grave heresy. But I doubt whether my opinion will carry much weight with the orthodox.

It was only very slowly and reluctantly that the church sanctioned the dissection of corpses in connection with the study of medicine. The pioneer in dissection was Vesalius, who was Court physician to the Emperor Charles V. His medical skill led the Emperor to protect him, but after the Emperor was dead he got into trouble. A corpse which he was dissecting was said to have shown signs of life under the knife, and he was accused of murder. The Inquisition was induced by King Philip II to take a lenient view, and only sentenced him to a pilgrimage to the Holy Land. On the way home he was shipwrecked and died of exhaustion. For centuries after this time, medical students at the Papal University in Rome were only allowed to operate on lay figures, from which the sexual parts were omitted.

The sacredness of corpses is a widespread belief. It was carried furthest by the Egyptians, among whom it led to the practice of mummification. It still exists in full force in China. A French surgeon who was employed by the Chinese to teach Western medicine relates that his demand for corpses to dissect was received with horror, but he was assured that he could have instead an unlimited supply of live criminals. His objection to this alternative was totally unintelligible to his Chinese employers.

Although there are many kinds of sin, seven of which are deadly, the most fruitful field for Satan's wiles is sex. The orthodox Catholic doctrine on this subject is to be found in St. Paul, St. Augustine, and St. Thomas Aquinas. It is best to be celibate, but those who have not the gift of continence may marry. Intercourse in marriage is not sin, provided it is motivated by desire for offspring. All intercourse outside marriage is sin, and so is intercourse within marriage if any measures are adopted to prevent conception. Interruption of pregnancy is sin, even if, in medical opinion, it is the only way of saving the mother's life; for medical opinion is fallible, and God can always save a life by miracle if He sees fit. (This view is embodied in the law of Connecticut.) Venereal disease is God's punishment for sin. It is true that, through a guilty husband, this punishment may fall on an innocent woman and her children, but this is a mysterious dispensation of Providence which it would be impious to question. We must also not inquire why venereal disease was not divinely instituted until the time of Columbus. Since it is the appointed penalty for sin, all measures for its avoidance are also sin—except, of course, a virtuous life. Marriage is nominally indissoluble, but many people who seem to be married are not. In the case of influential Catholics, some ground for nullity can often be found, but for the poor there is no such outlet, except perhaps in cases of impotence. Persons who divorce and remarry are guilty of adultery in the sight of God.

The phrase "in the sight of God" puzzles me. One would suppose that God sees everything, but apparently this is a mistake. He does not see Reno, for you cannot be divorced in the sight of God. Register offices are a doubtful point. I notice that respectable people, who would not call on anybody who lives in open sin, are quite willing to call on people who have had only a civil marriage; so apparently God does see register offices.

Some eminent men think even the doctrine of the Catholic church deplorably lax where sex is concerned. Tolstoy and Mahatma Gandhi, in their old age, laid it down that *all* sexual intercourse is wicked, even in marriage and with a view to offspring. The Manicheans thought likewise, relying upon men's native sinfulness to supply them with a continually fresh crop of disciples. This doctrine, however, is heretical, though it is equally heretical to maintain that marriage is as praiseworthy as celibacy. Tolstoy thinks tobacco almost as bad as sex; in one of his novels, a man who is contemplating murder smokes a cigarette first in order to generate the necessary homicidal fury. Tobacco, however, is not prohibited in the Scriptures, though, as Samuel Butler points out, St. Paul would no doubt have denounced it if he had known of it.

It is odd that neither the church nor modern public opinion condemns petting, provided it stops short at a certain point. At what point sin begins is a matter as to which casuists differ. One eminently orthodox Catholic divine laid it down that a confessor may fondle a nun's breasts, provided he does it without evil intent. But I doubt whether modern authorities would agree with him on this point.

Modern morals are a mixture of two elements: on the one hand, rational precepts as to how to live together peaceably in a society, and on the other hand traditional taboos derived originally from some ancient superstition, but proximately from sacred books, Christian, Mohammedan, Hindu, or Buddhist. To some extent the two agree; the prohibition of murder and theft, for instance, is supported both by human reason and by Divine command. But the prohibition of pork or beef has only scriptural authority, and that only in certain religions. It is odd that modern men, who are aware of what science has done in the way of bringing new knowledge and altering the conditions of social life, should still be willing to accept the authority of texts embodying the outlook of very ancient and very ignorant pastoral or agricultural tribes. It is discouraging that many of the precepts whose sacred character is thus uncritically acknowledged should be such as to inflict much wholly unnecessary misery. If men's kindly impulses were stronger, they would find some way of explaining that these precepts are not to be taken literally, any more than the command to "sell all that thou hast and give to the poor."

There are logical difficulties in the notion of Sin. We are

told that Sin consists in disobedience to God's commands, but we are also told that God is omnipotent. If He is, nothing contrary to His will can occur; therefore when the sinner disobeys His commands, He must have intended this to happen. St. Augustine boldly accepts this view, and asserts that men are led to sin by a blindness with which God afflicts them. But most theologians, in modern times, have felt that, if God causes men to sin, it is not fair to send them to hell for what they cannot help. We are told that sin consists in acting contrary to God's will. This, however, does not get rid of the difficulty. Those who, like Spinoza, take God's omnipotence seriously, deduce that there can be no such thing as sin. This leads to frightful results. What! said Spinoza's contemporaries, was it not wicked of Nero to murder his mother? Was it not wicked of Adam to eat the apple? Is one action just as good as another? Spinoza wriggles, but does not find any satisfactory answer. *If* everything happens in accordance with God's will, God must have wanted Nero to murder his mother; therefore, since God is good, the murder must have been a good thing. From this argument there is no escape.

On the other hand, those who are in earnest in thinking that sin is disobedience to God are compelled to say that God is not omnipotent. This gets out of all the logical puzzles, and is the view adopted by a certain school of liberal theologians. It has, however, its own difficulties. How are we to know what really is God's will? If the forces of evil have a certain share of power, they may deceive us into accepting as Scripture what is really their work. This was the view of the Gnostics, who thought that the Old Testament was the work of an evil spirit.

As soon as we abandon our own reason, and are content to rely upon authority, there is no end to our troubles. Whose authority? The Old Testament? The New Testament? The

Koran? In practice, people choose the book considered sacred by the community in which they are born, and out of that book they choose the parts they like, ignoring the others. At one time, the most influential text in the Bible was: "Thou shalt not suffer a witch to live." Nowadays, people pass over this text, in silence if possible; if not, with an apology. And so, even when we have a sacred book, we still choose as truth whatever suits our own prejudices. No Catholic, for instance, takes seriously the text which says that a Bishop should be the husband of one wife.

People's beliefs have various causes. One is that there is some evidence for the belief in question. We apply this to matters of fact, such as "what is so-and-so's telephone number?" or "who won the World Series?" But as soon as it comes to anything more debatable, the causes of belief become less defensible. We believe, first and foremost, what makes us feel that we are fine fellows. Mr. Homo, if he has a good digestion and a sound income, thinks to himself how much more sensible he is than his neighbor so-and-so, who married a flighty wife and is always losing money. He thinks how superior his city is to the one fifty miles away: it has a bigger Chamber of Commerce and a more enterprising Rotary Club, and its mayor has never been in prison. He thinks how immeasurably his country surpasses all others. If he is an Englishman, he thinks of Shakespeare and Milton, or of Newton and Darwin, or of Nelson and Wellington, according to his temperament. If he is a Frenchman, he congratulates himself on the fact that for centuries France has led the world in culture, fashions, and cookery. If he is a Russian, he reflects that he belongs to the only nation which is truly international. If he is a Yugoslav, he boasts of his nation's pigs; if a native of the Principality of Monaco, he boasts of leading the world in the matter of gambling.

But these are not the only matters on which he has to congratulate himself. For is he not an individual of the species *homo sapiens?* Alone among animals he has an immortal soul, and is rational; he knows the difference between good and evil, and has learned the multiplication table. Did not God make him in His own image? And was not everything created for man's convenience? The sun was made to light the day, and the moon to light the night—though the moon, by some oversight, only shines during half the nocturnal hours. The raw fruits of the earth were made for human sustenance. Even the white tails of rabbits, according to some theologians, have a purpose, namely to make it easier for sportsmen to shoot them. There are, it is true, some inconveniences: lions and tigers are too fierce, the summer is too hot, and the winter too cold. But these things only began after Adam ate the apple; before that, all animals were vegetarians, and the season was always spring. If only Adam had been content with peaches and nectarines, grapes and pears and pineapples, these blessings would still be ours.

Self-importance, individual or generic, is the source of most of our religious beliefs. Even Sin is a conception derived from self-importance. Borrow relates how he met a Welsh preacher who was always melancholy. By sympathetic questioning he was brought to confess the source of his sorrow: that at the age of seven he had committed the Sin against the Holy Ghost. "My dear fellow," said Borrow, "don't let that trouble you; I know dozens of people in like case. Do not imagine yourself cut off from the rest of mankind by this occurrence; if you inquire, you will find multitudes who suffer from the same misfortune." From that moment, the man was cured. He had enjoyed feeling singular, but there was no pleasure in being one of a herd of sinners. Most sinners are rather less egotistical; but theologians undoubtedly enjoy the feeling that

Man is the special object of God's wrath, as well as of His love. After the Fall, so Milton assures us—

> The Sun
> Had first his precept so to move, so to shine,
> As might affect the Earth with cold and heat
> Scarce tolerable, and from the North to call
> Decrepit Winter, from the South to bring
> Solstitial summer's heat.

However disagreeable the results may have been, Adam could hardly help feeling flattered that such vast astronomical phenomena should be brought about to teach *him* a lesson. The whole of theology, in regard to hell no less than to heaven, takes it for granted that Man is what is of most importance in the Universe of created beings. Since all theologians are men, this postulate has met with little opposition.

Since evolution became fashionable, the glorification of Man has taken a new form. We are told that evolution has been guided by one great Purpose: through the millions of years when there were only slime, or trilobites, throughout the ages of dinosaurs and giant ferns, of bees and wild flowers, God was preparing the Great Climax. At last, in the fullness of time, He produced Man, including such specimens as Nero and Caligula, Hitler and Mussolini, whose transcendent glory justified the long painful process. For my part, I find even eternal damnation less incredible, and certainly less ridiculous, than this lame and impotent conclusion which we are asked to admire as the supreme effort of Omnipotence. And if God is indeed omnipotent, why could He not have produced the glorious result without such a long and tedious prologue?

Apart from the question whether Man is really so glorious as the theologians of evolution say he is, there is the further difficulty that life on this planet is almost certainly temporary. The earth will grow cold, or the atmosphere will gradually fly off, or there will be an insufficiency of water, or, as Sir

James Jeans genially prophesies, the sun will burst and all the
planets will be turned into gas. Which of those will happen
first, no one knows; but in any case the human race will ultimately die out. Of course, such an event is of little importance
from the point of view of orthodox theology, since men are
immortal, and will continue to exist in heaven and hell when
none are left on earth. But in that case why bother about
terrestrial developments? Those who lay stress on the gradual
progress from the primitive slime to Man attach an importance
to this mundane sphere which should make them shrink from
the conclusion that all life on earth is only a brief interlude between the nebula and the eternal frost, or perhaps between one
nebula and another. The importance of Man, which is the one
indispensable dogma of the theologians, receives no support
from a scientific view of the future of the solar system.

There are many other sources of false belief besides self-
importance. One of these is love of the marvelous. I knew at
one time a scientifically minded conjuror, who used to perform
his tricks before a small audience, and then get them, each
separately, to write down what they had seen happen. Almost
always they wrote down something much more astonishing
than the reality, and usually something which no conjuror
could have achieved; yet they all thought they were reporting
truly what they had seen with their own eyes. This sort of
falsification is still more true of rumors. A tells B that last
night he saw Mr. ——, the eminent prohibitionist, slightly the
worse for liquor; B tells C that A saw the good man reeling
drunk, C tells D that he was picked up unconscious in the
ditch, D tells E that he is well known to pass out every
evening. Here, it is true, another motive comes in, namely
malice. We like to think ill of our neighbors, and are prepared to believe the worst on very little evidence. But even
where there is no such motive, what is marvelous is readily
believed unless it goes against some strong prejudice. All his-

tory until the eighteenth century is full of prodigies and wonders which modern historians ignore, not because they are less well attested than facts which the historians accept, but because modern taste among the learned prefers what science regards as probable. Shakespeare relates how on the night before Caesar was killed,

> A common slave—you know him well by sight—
> Held up his left hand, which did flame and burn
> Like twenty torches join'd; and yet his hand,
> Not sensible of fire, remain'd unscorch'd.
> Besides—I have not since put up my sword—
> Against the Capitol I met a lion,
> Who glar'd upon me, and went surly by,
> Without annoying me; and there were drawn
> Upon a heap a hundred ghastly women,
> Transformed with their fear, who swore they saw
> Men all in fire walk up and down the streets.

Shakespeare did not invent these marvels; he found them in reputable historians, who are among those upon whom we depend for our knowledge concerning Julius Caesar. This sort of thing always used to happen at the death of a great man or the beginning of an important war. Even so recently as 1914 the "angels of Mons" encouraged the British troops. The evidence for such events is very seldom first-hand, and modern historians refuse to accept it—except, of course, where the event is one that has religious importance.

Every powerful emotion has its own myth-making tendency. When the emotion is peculiar to an individual, he is considered more or less mad if he gives credence to such myths as he has invented. But when an emotion is collective, as in war, there is no one to correct the myths that naturally arise. Consequently in all times of great collective excitement unfounded rumors obtain wide credence. In September, 1914, almost everybody in England believed that Russian troops had passed through England on the way to the Western Front. Everybody knew someone who had seen them, though no one had seen them himself.

This myth-making faculty is often allied with cruelty. Ever since the middle ages, the Jews have been accused of practicing ritual murder. There is not an iota of evidence for this accusation, and no sane person who has examined it believes it. Nevertheless it persists. I have met White Russians who were convinced of its truth, and among many Nazis it was accepted without question. Such myths give an excuse for the infliction of torture, and the unfounded belief in them is evidence of the unconscious desire to find some victim to persecute.

There was, until the end of the eighteenth century, a theory that insanity is due to possession by devils. It was inferred that any pain suffered by the patient is also suffered by the devils, so that the best cure is to make the patient suffer so much that the devils will decide to abandon him. The insane, in accordance with this theory, were savagely beaten. This treatment was tried on King George III when he was mad, but without success. It is a curious and painful fact that almost all the completely futile treatments that have been believed in during the long history of medical folly have been such as caused acute suffering to the patient. When anaesthetics were discovered pious people considered them an attempt to evade the will of God. It was pointed out, however, that when God extracted Adam's rib He put him into a deep sleep. This proved that anaesthetics are all right for *men;* women, however, ought to suffer because of the curse of Eve. In the West votes for women proved this doctrine mistaken, but in Japan, to this day, women in childbirth are not allowed any alleviation through anaesthetics. As the Japanese do not believe in Genesis, this piece of sadism must have some other justification.

The fallacies about "race" and "blood," which have always been popular, and which the Nazis embodied in their official creed, have no objective justification; they are believed solely because they minister to self-esteem and to the impulse toward cruelty. In one form or another, these beliefs are as old as civilization; their forms change, but their essence remains. Herodotus tells how Cyrus was brought up by peasants, in complete ignorance of his royal blood; at the age of 12, his kingly bearing toward other peasant boys revealed the truth. This is a variant of an old story which is found in all Indo-European countries. Even quite modern people say that "blood will tell." It is no use for scientific physiologists to assure the world that there is no difference between the blood of a Negro and the blood of a white man. The American Red Cross, in obedience to popular prejudice, at first, when America became involved in the last war, decreed that no Negro blood should be used for blood transfusion. As a result of an agitation, it was conceded that Negro blood might be used, but only for Negro patients. Similarly, in Germany, the Aryan soldier who needed blood transfusion was carefully protected from the contamination of Jewish blood.

In the matter of race, there are different beliefs in different societies. Where monarchy is firmly established, kings are of a higher race than their subjects. Until very recently, it was universally believed that men are congenitally more intelligent than women; even so enlightened a man as Spinoza decides against votes for women on this ground. Among white men, it is held that white men are by nature superior to men of other colors, and especially to black men; in Japan, on the contrary, it is thought that yellow is the best color. In Haiti, when they make statues of Christ and Satan, they make Christ black and Satan white. Aristotle and Plato considered Greeks so innately superior to barbarians that slavery is justified so long as the master is Greek and the slave barbarian. The American legislators who made the immigration laws consider the Nordics superior to Slavs or Latins or any other white men. But the Nazis, under the stress of war, were led to the conclusion that there are hardly any true Nordics outside Germany; the Norwegians, except Quisling and his few followers, had been corrupted by intermixture with Finns and Lapps and such. Thus politics are a clue to descent. The biologically pure Nordics love Hitler, and if you did not love Hitler, that was proof of tainted blood.

All this is, of course, pure nonsense, known to be such by everyone who has studied the subject. In schools in America, children of the most diverse origins are subjected to the same educational system, and those whose business it is to measure intelligence quotients and otherwise estimate the native ability of students are unable to make any such racial distinctions as are postulated by the theorists of race. In every national or racial group there are clever children and stupid children. It is not likely that, in the United States, colored children will develop as successfully as white children, because of the stigma of social inferiority; but in so far as congenital ability can be detached from environmental influence, there is no clear distinction among different groups. The whole conception of superior races is merely a myth generated by the overweening self-esteem of the holders of power. It may be that, some day, better evidence will be forthcoming; perhaps, in time, educators will be able to prove (say) that Jews are on the average more intelligent than gentiles. But as yet no such evidence exists, and all talk of superior races must be dismissed as nonsense.

There is a special absurdity in applying racial theories to the various populations of Europe. There is not in Europe any such thing as a pure race. Russians have an admixture of Tartar blood, Germans are largely Slavonic, France is a mixture of Celts, Germans, and people of Mediterranean race, Italy the same with the addition of the descendants of slaves imported by the Romans. The English are perhaps the most mixed of all. There is no evidence that there is any advantage in belonging to a pure race. The purest races now in existence are the Pygmies, the Hottentots, and the Australian aborigines; the Tasmanians, who were probably even purer, are extinct. They were not the bearers of a brilliant culture. The ancient Greeks, on the other hand, emerged from an amalgamation of northern barbarians and an indigenous population; the Athenians and Ionians, who were the most civilized, were also the most mixed. The supposed merits of racial purity are, it would seem, wholly imaginary.

Superstitions about blood have many forms that have noth-ing to do with race. The objection to homicide seems to have been, originally, based on the ritual pollution caused by the blood of the victim. God said to Cain: "The voice of thy brother's blood crieth unto me from the ground." According to some anthropologists, the mark of Cain was a disguise to prevent Abel's blood from finding him; this appears also to be the original reason for wearing mourning. In many ancient communities no difference was made between murder and accidental homicide; in either case equally ritual ablution was necessary. The feeling that blood defiles still lingers, for ex-ample in the Churching of Women and in taboos connected with menstruation. The idea that a child is of his father's "blood" has the same superstitious origin. So far as actual blood is concerned, the blood of neither father nor mother enters the child. The importance attached to blood before the discovery of genes is therefore a superstition.

In Russia, where, under the influence of Karl Marx, people since the revolution have been classified by their economic origin, difficulties have arisen not unlike those of German race theorists over the Scandinavian Nordics. There were two theories that had to be reconciled: on the one hand, prole-tarians were good and other people were bad; on the other hand, Communists were good and other people were bad. The only way of effecting a reconciliation was to alter the meaning of words. A "proletarian" came to mean a supporter of the government; Lenin, though born a noble, was reckoned a member of the proletariat. On the other hand, the word "kulak," which was supposed to mean a rich peasant, came to mean any peasant who opposed collectivization. This sort of absurdity always arises when one group of human beings is supposed to be inherently better than another. In America, the highest praise that can be bestowed on an eminent colored man after he is safely dead is to say "he was a *white* man." A courageous woman is called "masculine"; Macbeth, praising his wife's courage, says:

> Bring forth men children only,
> For thy undaunted mettle should compose
> Nothing but males.

All these ways of speaking come of unwillingness to abandon foolish generalizations.

In the economic sphere there are many widespread superstitions.

Why do people value gold and precious stones? Not simply because of their rarity: there are a number of elements called "rare earths" which are much rarer than gold, but no one will give a penny for them except a few men of science. There is a theory, for which there is much to be said, that gold and gems were valued originally on account of their supposed magical properties. The mistakes of governments in modern times seem to show that this belief still exists among the sort of men who are called "practical." At the end of the 1914–18 war, it was agreed that Germany should pay vast sums to England and France, and they in turn should pay vast sums to the United States. Every one wanted to be paid in money rather than goods; the "practical" men failed to notice that there is not that amount of money in the world. They also failed to notice that money is no use unless it is used to buy goods. As they would not use it in this way, it did no good

to anyone. There was supposed to be some mystic virtue about
gold that made it worth while to dig it up in the Transvaal and
put it underground again in bank vaults in America. In the
end, of course, the debtor countries had no more money, and,
since they were not allowed to pay in goods, they went bank-
rupt. The great depression was the direct result of the surviving belief in the magical properties of gold. This superstition
now seems dead, but no doubt others will replace it.

Politics is largely governed by sententious platitudes which
are devoid of truth.

One of the most widespread popular maxims is, "Human
nature cannot be changed." No one can say whether this is
true or not without first defining "human nature." But as used
it is certainly false. When Mr. A utters the maxim, with an air
of portentous and conclusive wisdom, what he means is that
all men everywhere will always continue to behave as they do
in his own home town. A little anthropology will dispel this
belief. Among the Tibetans, one wife has many husbands,
because men are too poor to support a whole wife; yet family
life, according to travelers, is no more unhappy than elsewhere. The practice of lending one's wife to a guest is very
common among uncivilized tribes. The Australian aborigines,
at puberty, undergo a very painful operation which, throughout the rest of their lives, greatly diminishes sexual potency.
Infanticide, which might seem contrary to human nature, was
almost universal before the rise of Christianity, and is recom-
mended by Plato to prevent over-population. Private property
is not recognized among some savage tribes. Even among highly
civilized people, economic considerations will override what
is called "human nature." In Moscow, where there is an acute
housing shortage, when an unmarried women is pregnant, it
often happens that a number of men contend for the legal right
to be considered the father of the prospective child, because

whoever is judged to be the father acquires the right to share the woman's room, and half a room is better than no roof.

In fact, adult "human nature" is extremely variable, according to the circumstances of education. Food and sex are very general requirements, but the hermits of the Thebaid eschewed sex altogether and reduced food to the lowest point compatible with survival. By diet and training, people can be made ferocious or meek, masterful or slavish, as may suit the educator. There is no nonsense so arrant that it cannot be made the creed of the vast majority by adequate governmental action. Plato intended his Republic to be founded on a myth which he admitted to be absurd, but he was rightly confident that the populace could be induced to believe it. Hobbes, who thought it important that people should reverence the government however unworthy it might be, meets the argument that it might be difficult to obtain general assent to anything so irrational by pointing out that people have been brought to believe in the Christian religion, and, in particular, in the dogma of transubstantiation. If he had been alive in 1940, he would have found ample confirmation of his contention in the devotion of German youth to the Nazis.

The power of governments over men's beliefs has been very great ever since the rise of large states. The great majority of Romans became Christian after the Roman Emperors had been converted. In the parts of the Roman Empire that were conquered by the Arabs, most people abandoned Christianity for Islam. The division of Western Europe into Protestant and Catholic regions was determined by the attitude of governments in the sixteenth century. But the power of governments over belief in the present day is vastly greater than at any earlier time. A belief, however untrue, is important when it dominates the actions of large masses of men. In this sense, the beliefs inculcated before the last war by the Japanese, Russian, and German governments were important. Since they were completely divergent, they could not all be true, though they could well all be false. Unfortunately, they were such as to inspire men with an ardent desire to kill one another, even to the point of almost completely inhibiting the impulse of self-preservation. No one can deny, in face of the evidence, that it is easy, given military power, to produce a population of fanatical lunatics. It would be equally easy to produce a population of sane and reasonable people, but many governments do not wish to do so, since such people would fail to admire the politicians who are at the head of these governments.

There is one peculiarly pernicious application of the doctrine that human nature cannot be changed. This is the dogmatic assertion that there will always be wars, because we are so constituted that we feel a need of them. What is true is that a man who has had the kind of diet and education that most men have will wish to fight when provoked. But he will not actually fight unless he has a chance of victory. It is very annoying to be stopped by a policeman, but we do not fight him because we know that he has the overwhelming forces of the state at his back. People who have no occasion for war do not make any impression of being psychologically thwarted. Sweden has had no war since 1814, but the Swedes are one of the happiest and most contented nations in the world. The only cloud upon their national happiness is fear of being involved in the next war. If political organization were such as to make war obviously unprofitable, there is nothing in human nature that would compel its occurrence, or make average people unhappy because of its not occurring. Exactly the same arguments that are now used about the impossibility of preventing war were formerly used in defense of dueling, yet few of us feel thwarted because we are not allowed to fight duels.

I am persuaded that there is absolutely no limit to the

absurdities that can, by government action, come to be generally believed. Give me an adequate army, with power to provide it with more pay and better food than falls to the lot of the average man, and I will undertake, within 30 years, to make the majority of the population believe that two and two are three, that water freezes when it gets hot and boils when it gets cold, or any other nonsense that might seem to serve the interest of the state. Of course, even when these beliefs had been generated, people would not put the kettle in the refrigerator when they wanted it to boil. That cold makes water boil would be a Sunday truth, sacred and mystical, to be professed in awed tones, but not to be acted on in daily life. What would happen would be that any verbal denial of the mystic doctrine would be made illegal, and obstinate heretics would be "frozen" at the stake. No person who did not enthusiastically accept the official doctrine would be allowed to teach or to have any position of power. Only the very highest officials, in their cups, would whisper to each other what rubbish it all is; then they would laugh and drink again. This is hardly a caricature of what happens under some modern governments.

The discovery that man can be scientifically manipulated, and that governments can turn large masses this way or that as they choose, is one of the causes of our misfortunes. There is as much difference between a collection of mentally free citizens and a community molded by modern methods of propaganda as there is between a heap of raw materials and a battleship. Education, which was at first made universal in order that all might be able to read and write, has been found capable of serving quite other purposes. By instilling nonsense it unifies populations and generates collective enthusiasm. If all governments taught the same nonsense, the harm would not be so great. Unfortunately each has its own brand, and the diversity serves to produce hostility between the devotees of different creeds. If there is ever to be peace in the world, governments will have to agree either to inculcate no dogmas, or all to inculcate the same. The former, I fear, is a Utopian ideal, but perhaps they could agree to teach collectively that all public men, everywhere, are completely virtuous and perfectly wise. Perhaps, after the next war, the surviving politicians may find it prudent to combine on some such program.

But if conformity has it dangers, so has nonconformity.

Some "advanced thinkers" are of opinion that anyone who differs from the conventional opinion must be in the right. This is a delusion; if it were not, truth would be easier to come by than it is. There are infinite possibilities of error, and more cranks take up unfashionable errors than unfashionable truths. I met once an electrical engineer whose first words to men were: "How do you do. There are two methods of faith-healing, the one practiced by Christ and the one practiced by most Christian Scientists. I practice the method practiced by Christ." Shortly afterwards, he was sent to prison for making out fraudulent balance-sheets. The law does not look kindly on the intrusion of faith into this region. I knew also an eminent lunacy doctor who took to philosophy, and taught a new logic which, as he frankly confessed, he had learned from his lunatics. When he died he left a will founding a professorship for the teaching of his new scientific methods, but unfortunately he left no assets. Arithmetic proved recalcitrant to lunatic logic. On one occasion a man came to ask me to recommend some of my books, as he was interested in philosophy. I did so, but he returned next day saying that he had been reading one of them, and had found only one statement he could understand, and that one seemed to him false. I asked him what it was, and he said it was the statement that Julius Caesar is dead. When I asked him why he did not agree, he drew himself up and said: "Because I am Julius Caesar." These examples may suffice to show that you cannot make sure of being right by being eccentric.

Science, which has always had to fight its way against popular beliefs, now has one of its most difficult battles in the sphere of psychology.

People who think they know all about human nature are always hopelessly at sea when they have to do with any abnormality. Some boys never learn to be what, in animals, is called "house-trained." The sort of person who won't stand any nonsense deals with such cases by punishment; the boy is beaten, and when he repeats the offense he is beaten worse. All medical men who have studied the matter know that punishment only aggravates the trouble. Sometimes the cause is physical, but usually it is psychological, and only curable by removing some deep-seated and probably unconscious grievance. But most people enjoy punishing anyone who irritates them, and so the medical view is rejected as fancy nonsense. The same sort of thing applies to men who are exhibitionists; they are sent to prison over and over again, but as soon as they come out they repeat the offense. A medical man who specialized in such ailments assured me that the exhibitionist can be cured by the simple device of having trousers that button up the back instead of the front. But this method is not tried because it does not satisfy people's vindictive impulses.

Broadly speaking, punishment is likely to prevent crimes that are sane in origin, but not those that spring from some psychological abnormality. This is now partially recognized; we distinguish between plain theft, which springs from what may be called rational self-interest, and kleptomania, which is a mark of something queer. And homicidal maniacs are not treated like ordinary murderers. But sexual aberrations rouse so much disgust that it is still impossible to have them treated medically rather than punitively. Indignation, though on the whole a useful social force, becomes harmful when it is directed against the victims of maladies that only medical skill can cure.

The same sort of thing happens as regards whole nations. During the 1914–18 war, very naturally, people's vindictive feelings were aroused against the Germans, who were severely punished after their defeat. During the second war it was argued that the Versailles Treaty was ridiculously mild, since it failed to teach a lesson; this time, we were told, there must be *real* severity. To my mind, we should have been more likely to prevent a repetition of German aggression if we had regarded the rank and file of the Nazis as we regard lunatics than by thinking of them as merely and simply criminals. Lunatics, of course, have to be restrained. But lunatics are restrained from prudence, not as a punishment, and so far as prudence permits we try to make them happy. Everybody recognizes that a homicidal maniac will only become more homicidal if he is made miserable. There were, of course, many men among the Nazis who were plain criminals, but there must also have been many who were more or less mad. If Germany is to be successfully incorporated in Western Europe, there must be a complete abandonment of all attempt to instill a feeling of special guilt. Those who are being punished seldom learn to feel kindly towards the men who punish them. And so long as the Germans hate the rest of mankind peace will be precarious.

When one reads of the beliefs of savages, or of the ancient Babylonians and Egyptians, they seem surprising by their capricious absurdity. But beliefs that are just as absurd are still entertained by the uneducated even in the most modern and civilized societies. I have been gravely assured, in America, that people born in March are unlucky and people born in May are peculiarly liable to corns. I do not know the history of these superstitions, but probably they are derived from Babylonian or Egyptian priestly lore. Beliefs begin the higher social strata, and then, like mud in a river, sink gradually downwards in the educational scale; they may take 3,000 or 4,000 years to sink all the way. In America you may find your colored maid making some remark that comes straight out of Plato—not the parts of Plato that scholars quote, but the parts where he utters obvious nonsense, such as that men who do not pursue wisdom in this life will be born again as women. Commentators on great philosophers always politely ignore their silly remarks.

Aristotle, in spite of his reputation, is full of absurdities. He says that children should be conceived in the winter, when the wind is in the north, and that if people marry too young the children will be female. He tells us that the blood of females is blacker than that of males; that the pig is the only animal liable to measles; that an elephant suffering from insomnia should have its shoulders rubbed with salt, olive oil, and warm water; that women have fewer teeth than men, and so on. Nevertheless, he is considered by the great majority of philosophers a paragon of wisdom.

Superstitions about lucky and unlucky days are almost universal. In ancient times they governed the actions of generals. Among ourselves the prejudice against Friday and the number 13 is very active; sailors do not like to sail on a Friday, and many hotels have no 13th floor. The superstitions about Friday and 13 were once believed by those reputed wise; now such men regard them as harmless follies. But probably 2,000 years hence many beliefs of the wise of our day will have come to seem equally foolish. Man is a credulous animal, and must believe *something;* in the absence of good grounds for belief, he will be satisfied with bad ones.

Belief in "nature" and what is "natural" is a source of many errors. It used to be, and to some extent still is, powerfully operative in medicine. The human body, left to itself, has a certain power of curing itself; small cuts usually heal, colds pass off, and even serious diseases sometimes disappear without medical treatment. But aids to nature are very desirable, even in these cases. Cuts may turn septic if not disinfected, colds may turn to pneumonia, and serious diseases are only left without treatment by explorers and travelers in remote regions, who have no option. Many practices which have come to seem "natural" were originally "unnatural," for instance clothing and washing. Before men adopted clothing they must have found it impossible to live in cold climates. Where there is not a modicum of cleanliness, populations suffer from various diseases, such as typhus, from which Western nations have become exempt. Vaccination was (and by some still is) objected to as "unnatural." But there is no consistency in such objections, for no one supposes that a broken bone can be mended by "natural" behavior. Eating cooked food is "unnatural"; so is heating our houses. The Chinese philosopher Lao-tse, whose traditional date is about 600 B.C., objected to roads and bridges and boats as "unnatural," and in his disgust at such mechanistic devices left China and went to live among the Western barbarians. Every advance in civilization has been denounced as unnatural while it was recent.

The commonest objection to birth control is that it is against "nature." (For some reason we are not allowed to say that celibacy is against nature; the only reason I can think of is that it is not new.) Malthus saw only three ways of keeping down the population: moral restraint, vice, and misery. Moral restraint, he admitted, was not likely to be practiced on a large scale. "Vice," i.e. birth control, he, as a clergyman, viewed with abhorrence. There remained misery. In his comfortable parsonage, he contemplated the misery of the great majority of mankind with equanimity, and pointed out the fallacies of the reformers who hoped to alleviate it. Modern theological opponents of birth control are less honest. They pretend to think that God will provide, however many mouths there may be to feed. They ignore the fact that He has never done so hitherto, but has left mankind exposed to periodical famines in which millions died of hunger. They must be deemed to hold —if they are saying what they believe—that from this moment onwards God will work a continual miracle of loaves and fishes which He has hitherto thought unnecessary. Or perhaps they will say that suffering here below is of no importance; what matters is the hereafter. By their own theology, most of the children whom their opposition to birth control will cause to exist will go to hell. We must suppose, therefore, that they oppose the amelioration of life on earth because they think it a good thing that many millions should suffer eternal torment. By comparison with them, Malthus appears merciful.

Women, as the object of our strongest love and aversion, rouse complex emotions which are embodied in proverbial "wisdom."

Almost everybody allows himself or herself some entirely unjustifiable generalization on the subject of Woman. Married men, when they generalize on that subject, judge by their wives; women judge by themselves. It would be amusing to write a history of men's views on women. In antiquity, when male supremacy was unquestioned and Christian ethics were still unknown, women were harmless but rather silly, and a man who took them seriously was somewhat despised. Plato thinks it a grave objection to the drama that the playwright has to imitate women in creating his female roles. With the coming of Christianity woman took on a new part, that of the temptress; but at the same time she was also found capable of being a saint. In Victorian days the saint was much more emphasized than the temptress; Victorian men could not admit themselves susceptible to temptation. The superior virtue of women was made a reason for keeping them out of politics, where, it was held, a lofty virtue is impossible. But the early feminists turned the argument round, and contended that the participation of women would ennoble politics. Since this has turned out to be an illusion, there has been less talk of women's superior virtue, but there are still a number of men who adhere to the monkish view of woman as the temptress. Women themselves, for the most part, think of themselves as the sensible sex, whose business it is to undo the harm that comes of men's impetuous follies. For my part I distrust *all* generalizations about women, favorable and unfavorable, masculine and feminine, ancient and modern; all alike, I should say, result from paucity of experience.

The deeply irrational attitude of each sex towards women may be seen in novels, particularly in bad novels. In bad novels by men, there is the woman with whom the author is in love, who usually possesses every charm, but is somewhat helpless, and requires male protection; sometimes, however, like Shakespeare's Cleopatra, she is an object of exasperated hatred, and is thought to be deeply and desperately wicked. In portraying the heroine, the male author does not write from observation, but merely objectifies his own emotions. In regard to his other female characters, he is more objective, and may even depend upon his notebook; but when he is in love, his passion makes a mist between him and the object of his devotion. Women novelists, also, have two kinds of women in their books. One is themselves, glamorous and kind, and object of lust to the wicked and of love to the good, sensitive, high-souled, and constantly misjudged. The other kind is represented by all other women, and is usually portrayed as petty, spiteful, cruel, and deceitful. It would seem that to judge women without bias is not easy either for men or for women.

Generalizations about national characteristics are just as common and just as unwarranted as generalizations about women. Until 1870, the Germans were thought of as a nation of spectacled professors, evolving everything out of their inner consciousness, and scarcely aware of the outer world, but since 1870 this conception has had to be very sharply revised.

Frenchmen seem to be thought of by most Americans as per-petually engaged in amorous intrigue; Walt Whitman, in one of his catalogues, speaks of "the adulterous French couple on the sly settee." Americans who go to live in France are aston-ished, and perhaps disappointed, by the intensity of family life. Before the Russian Revolution, the Russians were credited with a mystical Slav soul, which, while it incapacitated them for ordinary sensible behavior, gave them a kind of deep wis-dom to which more practical nations could not hope to attain. Suddenly everything was changed: mysticism was taboo, and only the most earthly ideals were tolerated. The truth is that what appears to one nation as the national character of another depends upon a few prominent individuals, or upon the class that happens to have power. For this reason, all generalizations on this subject are liable to be completely upset by any impor-tant political change.

To avoid the various foolish opinions to which mankind are prone, no superhuman genius is required. A few simple rules will keep you, not from *all* error, but from silly error.

If the matter is one that can be settled by observation, make the observation yourself. Aristotle could have avoided the mis-take of thinking that women have fewer teeth than men, by the simple device of asking Mrs. Aristotle to keep her mouth open while he counted. He did not do so because he thought he knew. Thinking that you know when in fact you don't is a fatal mistake, to which we are all prone. I believe myself that hedgehogs eat black beetles, because I have been told that they do; but if I were writing a book on the habits of hedgehogs, I should not commit myself until I had seen one enjoying this unappetizing diet. Aristotle, however, was less cautious. An-cient and medieval authors knew all about unicorns and sala-manders; not one of them thought it necessary to avoid dog-matic statements about them because he had never seen one of them.

Many matters, however, are less easily brought to the test of experience. If, like most of mankind, you have passionate convictions on many such matters, there are ways in which you can make yourself aware of your own bias. If an opinion contrary to your own makes you angry, that is a sign that you are subconsciously aware of having no good reason for thinking as you do. If someone maintains that two and two are five, or that Iceland is on the equator, you feel pity rather than anger, unless you know so little of arithmetic or geography that his opinion shakes your own contrary conviction. The most savage controversies are those about matters as to which there is no good evidence either way. Persecution is used in theology, not in arithmetic, because in arithmetic there is knowledge, but in theology there is only opinion. So whenever you find yourself getting angry about a difference of opinion, be on your guard; you will probably find, on examination, that your belief is going beyond what the evidence warrants.

A good way of ridding yourself of certain kinds of dogmatism is to become aware of opinions held in social circles different from your own. When I was young, I lived much outside my own country—in France, Germany, Italy, and the United States. I found this very profitable in diminishing the intensity of insular prejudice. If you cannot travel, seek out people with whom you disagree, and read a newspaper belonging to a party that is not yours. If the people and the newspaper seem mad, perverse, and wicked, remind yourself that you seem so to them. In this opinion both parties may be right, but they cannot both be wrong. This reflection should generate a certain caution.

Becoming aware of foreign customs, however, does not always have a beneficial effect. In the seventeenth century, when the Manchus conquered China, it was the custom among the Chinese for the women to have small feet, and among the Manchus for the men to wear pigtails. Instead of each dropping their own foolish custom, they each adopted the foolish custom of the other, and the Chinese continued to wear pigtails until they shook off the dominion of the Manchus in the revolution of 1911.

For those who have enough psychological imagination, it is a good plan to imagine an argument with a person having a different bias. This has one advantage, and only one, as compared with actual conversation with opponents; this one advantage is that the method is not subject to the same limitations of time and space. Mahatma Gandhi deplored railways and steamboats and machinery; he would have liked to undo the whole of the industrial revolution. You may never have an opportunity of actually meeting anyone who holds this opinion, because in Western countries most people take the advantage of modern technique for granted. But if you want to make sure that you are right in agreeing with the prevailing opinion, you will find it a good plan to test the arguments that occur to you by considering what Gandhi might have said in refutation of them. I have sometimes been led actually to change my mind as a result of this kind of imaginary dialogue, and, short of this, I have frequently found myself growing less dogmatic and cocksure through realizing the possible reasonableness of a hypothetical opponent.

Be very wary of opinions that flatter your self-esteem. Both men and women, nine times out of ten, are firmly convinced of the superior excellence of their own sex. There is abundant evidence on both sides. If you are a man, you can point out that most poets and men of science are male; if you are a woman, you can retort that so are most criminals. The question is inherently insoluble, but self-esteem conceals this from most people. We are all, whatever part of the world we come from, persuaded that our own nation is superior to all others. Seeing that each nation has its characteristic merits and demerits, we adjust our standard of values so as to make out that the merits possessed by our nation are the really important ones, while its demerits are comparatively trivial. Here, again, the rational man will admit that the question is one to which there is no demonstrably right answer. It is more difficult to deal with the self-esteem of man as man, because we cannot argue out the matter with some nonhuman mind. The only way I know of dealing with this general human conceit is to remind ourselves that man is a brief episode in the life of a small planet in a little corner of the universe, and that, for aught we know, other parts of the cosmos may contain beings as superior to ourselves as we are to jelly-fish.

Other passions besides self-esteem are common sources of error; of these perhaps the most important is fear. Fear sometimes operates directly, by inventing rumors of disaster in wartime, or by imagining objects of terror, such as ghosts; sometimes it operates indirectly, by creating belief in something comforting, such as the elixir of life, or heaven for ourselves and hell for our enemies. Fear has many forms—fear of death, fear of the dark, fear of the unknown, fear of the herd, and that vague generalized fear that comes to those who conceal from themselves their more specific terrors. Until you have admitted your own fears to yourself, and have guarded yourself by a difficult effort of will against their myth-making power, you cannot hope to think truly about many matters of great importance, especially those with which religious beliefs are concerned. Fear is the main source of superstition, and one of the main sources of cruelty. To conquer fear is the beginning of wisdom, in the pursuit of truth as in the endeavor after a worthy manner of life.

There are two ways of avoiding fear: one is by persuading ourselves that we are immune from disaster, and the other is by the practice of sheer courage. The latter is difficult, and to everybody becomes impossible at a certain point. The former has therefore always been more popular. Primitive magic has the purpose of securing safety, either by injuring enemies, or by protecting oneself by talismans, spells, or incantations. Without any essential change, belief in such ways of avoiding danger survived throughout the many centuries of Babylonian civilization, spread from Babylon throughout the Empire of Alexander, and was acquired by the Romans in the course of their absorption of Hellenistic culture. From the Romans it descended to medieval Christendom and Islam. Science has now lessened the belief in magic, but many people place more faith in mascots than they are willing to avow, and sorcery, while condemned by the Church, is still officially a *possible* sin.

Magic, however, was a crude way of avoiding terrors, and, moreover, not a very effective way, for wicked magicians might always prove stronger than good ones. In the fifteenth, sixteenth, and seventeenth centuries, dread of witches and sorcerers led to the burning of hundreds of thousands convicted of these crimes. But newer beliefs, particularly as to the future life, sought more effective ways of combating fear. Socrates on the day of his death (if Plato is to be believed) expressed the conviction that in the next world he would live in the company of the gods and heroes, and surrounded by just spirits who would never object to his endless argumentation. Plato, in his *Republic*, laid it down that cheerful views of the next world must be enforced by the state, not because they were true, but to make soldiers more willing to die in battle. He would have none of the traditional myths about Hades, because they represented the spirits of the dead as unhappy.

Orthodox Christianity, in the Ages of Faith, laid down very definite rules for salvation. First, you must be baptized; then, you must avoid all theological error; last, you must, before dying, repent of your sins and receive absolution. All this would not save you from purgatory, but it would insure your ultimate arrival in heaven. It was not necessary to *know* theology. An eminent Cardinal stated authoritatively that the requirements of orthodoxy would be satisfied if you murmured on your deathbed: "I believe all that the Church believes; the Church believes all that I believe." These very definite directions ought to have made Catholics sure of finding the way to heaven. Nevertheless, the dread of hell persisted, and has caused, in recent times, a great softening of the dogmas as to who will be damned. The doctrine, professed by many modern Christians, that everybody will go to heaven, ought to do away with the fear of death, but in fact this fear is too instinctive to be easily vanquished. F. W. H. Myers, whom spiritualism had converted to belief in a future life, questioned a woman who had lately lost her daughter as to what she supposed had become of her soul. The mother replied: "Oh well, I suppose she is enjoying eternal bliss, but I wish you wouldn't talk about such unpleasant subjects." In spite of all that theology can do, heaven remains, to most people, an "unpleasant subject."

The most refined religions, such as those of Marcus Aurelius and Spinoza, are still concerned with the conquest of fear. The Stoic doctrine was simple: it maintained that the only true good is virtue, of which no enemy can deprive me; consequently, there is no need to fear enemies. The difficulty was that no one could really believe virtue to be the only good, not even Marcus Aurelius, who, as Emperor, sought not only to make his subjects virtuous, but to protect them against barbarians, pestilences, and famines. Spinoza taught a somewhat similar doctrine. According to him, our true good consists in indifference to our mundane fortunes. Both these men sought to escape from fear by pretending that such things as physical suffering are not really evil. This is a noble way of escaping from fear, but is still based upon false belief. And if genuinely accepted, it would have the bad effect of making men indifferent, not only to their own sufferings, but also to those of others.

Under the influence of great fear, almost everybody becomes superstitious. The sailors who threw Jonah overboard imagined his presence to be the cause of the storm which threatened to wreck their ship. In a similar spirit the Japanese, at the time of the Tokio earthquake, took to massacring Koreans and Liberals. When the Romans won victories in the Punic wars, the Carthaginians became persuaded that their misfortunes were due to a certain laxity which had crept into the worship of Moloch. Moloch liked having children sacrificed to him, and preferred them aristocratic; but the noble families of Carthage had adopted the practice of surreptitiously substituting plebeian children for their own offspring. This, it was thought, had displeased the god, and at the worst moments even the most aristocratic children were duly consumed in the fire. Strange to say, the Romans were victorious in spite of this democratic reform on the part of their enemies.

Collective fear stimulates herd instinct, and tends to produce ferocity towards those who are not regarded as members of the herd. So it was in the French Revolution, when dread of foreign armies produced the reign of terror. The Soviet government would have been less fierce if it had met with less hostility in its first years. Fear generates impulses of cruelty, and therefore promotes such superstitious beliefs as seem to justify cruelty. Neither a man nor a crowd nor a nation can be trusted to act humanely or to think sanely under the influence of a great fear. And for this reason poltroons are more prone to cruelty than brave men, and are also more prone to superstition. When I say this, I am thinking of men who are brave in all respects, not only in facing death. Many a man will have the courage to die gallantly, but will not have the courage to say, or even to think, that the cause for which he is asked to die is an unworthy one. Obloquy is, to most men, more painful than death; that is one reason why, in times of collective excitement, so few men venture to dissent from the prevailing opinion. No Carthaginian denied Moloch, because

to do so would have required more courage than was required
to face death in battle.

But we have been getting too solemn. Superstitions are not
always dark and cruel; often they add to the gaiety of life. I
received once a communication from the god Osiris, giving me
his telephone number; he lived, at that time, in a suburb of
Boston. Although I did not enroll myself among his worshipers, his letter gave me pleasure. I have frequently received
letters from men announcing themselves as the Messiah, and
urging me not to omit to mention this important fact in my
lectures. During prohibition in America, there was a sect
which maintained that the communion service ought to be
celebrated in whisky, not in wine; this tenet gave them a legal
right to a supply of hard liquor, and the sect grew rapidly.
There is in England a sect which maintains that the English
are the lost ten tribes; there is a stricter sect, which maintains
that they are only the tribes of Ephraim and Manasseh. Whenever I encounter a member of either of these sects, I profess
myself an adherent of the other, and much pleasant argumentation results. I like also the men who study the Great Pyramid,
with a view to deciphering its mystical lore. Many great books
have been written on this subject, some of which have been pre-
sented to me by their authors. It is a singular fact that the
Great Pyramid always predicts the history of the world ac-
curately up to the date of publication of the book in question,
but after that date it becomes less reliable. Generally the author
expects, very soon, wars in Egypt, followed by Armageddon
and the coming of Antichrist, but by this time so many people
have been recognized as Antichrist that the reader is reluctantly driven to skepticism.

I admire especially a certain prophetess who lived beside a
lake in northern New York State about the year 1820. She
announced to her numerous followers that she possessed the
power of walking on water, and that she proposed to do so at

II o'clock on a certain morning. At the stated time, the faithful assembled in their thousands beside the lake. She spoke to them saying: "Are you all entirely persuaded that I can walk on water?" With one voice they replied: "We are." "In that case," she announced, "there is no need for me to do so." And they all went home much edified.

Perhaps the world would lose some of its interest and variety if such beliefs were wholly replaced by cold science. Perhaps we may allow ourselves to be glad of the Abecedarians, who were so called because, having rejected all profane learning, they thought it wicked to learn the ABC. And we may enjoy the perplexity of the South American Jesuit who wondered how the sloth could have traveled, since the Flood, all the way from Mount Ararat to Peru—a journey which its extreme tardiness of locomotion rendered almost incredible. A wise man will enjoy the goods of which there is a plentiful supply, and of intellectual rubbish he will find an abundant diet, in our own age as in every other.

VIII

The Functions of a Teacher

TEACHING, more even than most other professions, has been transformed during the last hundred years from a small, highly skilled profession concerned with a minority of the population, to a large and important branch of the public service. The profession has a great and honorable tradition, extending from the dawn of history until recent times, but any teacher in the modern world who allows himself to be inspired by the ideals of his predecessors is likely to be made sharply aware that it is not his function to teach what he thinks, but to instill such beliefs and prejudices as are thought useful by his employers. In former days a teacher was expected to be a man of exceptional knowledge or wisdom, to whose words men would do well to attend. In antiquity, teachers were not an organized profession, and no control was exercised over what they taught. It is true that they were often punished afterwards for their subversive doctrines. Socrates was put to death and Plato is said to have been thrown into prison, but such incidents did not interfere with the spread of their doctrines. Any man who has the genuine impulse of the teacher will be more anxious to survive in his books than in the flesh. A feeling of intellectual independence is essential to the proper fulfillment of the teacher's functions, since it is his business to instill what he can of knowledge and reasonableness into the process of forming public opinion. In antiquity he performed this function unhampered except by occasional spasmodic and ineffective interventions of tyrants or mobs. In the middle ages teaching became the exclusive prerogative of the church, with the result that there was little progress either intellectual or social. With the Renaisssance, the general respect for learning brought back a very considerable measure of freedom to the teacher. It is true that the Inquisition compelled Galileo to recant, and burned Giordano Bruno at the stake, but each of these men had done his work before being punished. Institutions such as universities largely remained in the grip of the dogmatists, with the result that most of the best intellectual work was done by independent men of learning. In England, especially, until near the end of the nineteenth century, hardly any men of first-rate eminence except Newton were connected with universities. But the social system was such that this interfered little with their activities or their usefulness.

In our more highly organized world we face a new problem. Something called education is given to everybody, usually by the state, but sometimes by the churches. The teacher has thus become, in the vast majority of cases, a civil servant obliged to carry out the behests of men who have not his learning, who have no experience of dealing with the young, and whose only attitude towards education is that of the propagandist. It is not very easy to see how, in these circumstances, teachers can perform the functions for which they are specially fitted.

State education is obviously necessary, but as obviously involves certain dangers against which there ought to be safeguards. The evils to be feared were seen in their full magnitude in Nazi Germany and are still seen in Russia. Where these evils prevail no man can teach unless he subscribes to a dogmatic creed which few people of free intelligence are likely to accept sincerely. Not only must he subscribe to a creed, but he must condone abominations and carefully abstain from speaking his mind on current events. So long as he is teaching only the alphabet and the multiplication table, as to which no controversies arise, official dogmas do not necessarily warp his instruction; but even while he is teaching these elements he is expected, in totalitarian countries, not to employ the methods which he thinks most likely to achieve the scholastic result, but to instill fear, subservience, and blind obedience by demanding unquestioned submission to his authority. And as soon as he passes beyond the bare elements, he is obliged to take the official view on all controversial questions. The result is that the young in Nazi Germany became, and in Russia become, fanatical bigots, ignorant of the world outside their own country, totally unaccustomed to free discussion, and not aware that their opinions can be questioned without wickedness. This state of affairs, bad as it is, would be less disastrous than it is if the dogmas instilled were, as in medieval Catholicism, universal and international; but the whole conception of an international culture is denied by the modern dogmatists, who preached one creed in Germany, another in Italy, another in Russia, and yet another in Japan. In each of these countries fanatical nationalism was what was most emphasized in the teaching of the young, with the result that the men of one country have no common ground with the men of another, and that no conception of a common civilization stands in the way of warlike ferocity.

The decay of cultural internationalism has proceeded at a continually increasing pace ever since the First World War. When I was in Leningrad in 1920, I met the Professor of Pure Mathematics, who was familiar with London, Paris, and other capitals, having been a member of various international congresses. Nowadays the learned men of Russia are very seldom permitted such excursions, for fear of their drawing comparisons unfavorable to their own country. In other countries nationalism in learning is less extreme, but everywhere it is far more powerful than it was. There is a tendency in England (and, I believe, in the United States) to dispense with Frenchmen and Germans in the teaching of French and German. The practice of considering a man's nationality rather than his competence in appointing him to a post is damaging to education and an offense against the ideal of international culture, which was a heritage from the Roman Empire and the Catholic Church, but is now being submerged under a new barbarian invasion, proceeding from below rather than from without.

In democratic countries these evils have not yet reached anything like the same proportions, but it must be admitted that there is grave danger of similar developments in education, and that this danger can only be averted if those who believe in liberty of thought are on the alert to protect teachers from intellectual bondage. Perhaps the first requisite is a clear conception of the services which teachers can be expected to perform for the community. I agree with the governments of the world that the imparting of definite uncontroversial information is one of the least of the teacher's functions. It is, of course, the basis upon which the others are built, and in a technical civilization such as ours it has undoubtedly a considerable utility. There must exist in a modern community a sufficient number of men who possess the technical skill required to preserve the mechanical apparatus upon which our physical comforts depend. It is, moreover, inconvenient if any large percentage of the population is unable to read and write. For these reasons we are all in favor of universal compulsory education. But governments have perceived that it is easy, in the course of giving instruction, to instill beliefs on controversial matters and to produce habits of mind which may be convenient or inconvenient to those in authority. The defense of the state in all civilized countries is quite as much in the hands of teachers as in those of the armed forces. Except in totalitarian countries, the defense of the state is desirable, and the mere fact that education is used for this purpose is not in itself a ground of criticism. Criticism will only arise if the state is defended by obscurantism and appeals to irrational passion. Such methods are quite unnecessary in the case of any state worth defending. Nevertheless, there is a natural tendency towards their adoption by those who have no first-hand knowledge of education. There is a widespread belief that nations are made strong by uniformity of opinion and by the suppression of liberty. One hears it said over and over again that democracy weakens a country in war, in spite of the fact that in every important war since the year 1700 the victory has gone to the more democratic side. Nations have been brought to ruin much more often by insistence upon a narrow-minded doctrinal uniformity than by free discussion and the toleration of divergent opinions. Dogmatists the world over believe that although the truth is known to them, others will be led into false beliefs provided they are allowed to hear the arguments on both sides. This is a view which leads to one or another of two misfortunes: either one set of dogmatists conquers the world and prohibits all new ideas, or, what is worse, rival dogmatists conquer different regions and preach the gospel of hate against each other, the former of these evils existing in the middle ages, the latter during the wars of religion, and again in the present day. The first makes civilization static, the second tends to destroy it completely. Against both, the teacher should be the main safeguard.

It is obvious that organized party spirit is one of the greatest dangers of our time. In the form of nationalism it leads to wars between nations, and in other forms it leads to civil war. It should be the business of teachers to stand outside the strife of parties and endeavor to instill into the young the habit of impartial inquiry, leading them to judge issues on their merits and to be on their guard against accepting *ex parte* statements at their face value. The teacher should not be expected to flatter the prejudices either of the mob or of officials. His professional virtue should consist in a readiness to do justice to all sides, and in an endeavor to rise above controversy into a region of dispassionate scientific investigation. If there are people to whom the results of his investigation are inconvenient, he should be protected against their resentment, unless it can be shown that he has lent himself to dishonest propaganda by the dissemination of demonstrable untruths.

The function of the teacher, however, is not merely to mitigate the heat of current controversies. He has more positive tasks to perform, and he cannot be a great teacher unless he is inspired by a wish to perform these tasks. Teachers are more than any other class the guardians of civilization. They should be intimately aware of what civilization is, and desirous of imparting a civilized attitude to their pupils. We are thus brought to the question: what constitutes a civilized community?

This question would very commonly be answered by pointing to merely material tests. A country is civilized if it has much machinery, many motor cars, many bathrooms, and a great deal of rapid locomotion. To these things, in my opinion, most modern men attach much too much importance. Civilization, in the more important sense, is a thing of the mind, not of material adjuncts to the physical side of living. It is a matter partly of knowledge, partly of emotion. So far as knowledge is concerned, a man should be aware of the minuteness of himself and his immediate environment in relation to the world in time and space. He should see his own country not *only* as home, but as one among the countries of the world, all with an equal right to live and think and feel. He should see his own age in relation to the past and the future, and be aware that its own controversies will seem as strange to future ages as those of the past seem to us now. Taking an even wider view, he should be conscious of the vastness of geological epochs and astronomical abysses; but he should be aware of all this, not as a weight to crush the individual human spirit, but as a vast panorama which enlarges the mind that contemplates it. On the side of the emotions, a very similar enlargement from the purely personal is needed if a man is to be truly civilized. Men pass from birth to death, sometimes happy, sometimes un-happy; sometimes generous, sometimes grasping and petty; sometimes heroic, sometimes cowardly and servile. To the man who views the procession as a whole, certain things stand out as worthy of admiration. Some men have been inspired by love of mankind; some by supreme intellect have helped us to un-derstand the world in which we live; and some by exceptional sensitiveness have created beauty. These men have produced something of positive good to outweigh the long record of cruelty, oppression, and superstition. These men have done what lay in their power to make human life a better thing than the brief turbulence of savages. The civilized man, where he cannot admire, will aim rather at understanding than at repro-bating. He will seek rather to discover and remove the imper-sonal causes of evil than to hate the men who are in its grip. All this should be in the mind and heart of the teacher, and if it is in his mind and heart he will convey it in his teaching to the young who are in his care.

No man can be a good teacher unless he has feelings of warm affection towards his pupils and a genuine desire to im-part to them what he himself believes to be of value. This is not the attitude of the propagandist. To the propagandist his pupils are potential soldiers in an army. They are to serve pur-poses that lie outside their own lives, not in the sense in which every generous purpose transcends self, but in the sense of ministering to unjust privilege or to despotic power. The propagandist does not desire that his pupils should survey the world and freely choose a purpose which to them appears of value. He desires, like a topiarian artist, that their growth shall be trained and twisted to suit the gardener's purpose. And in thwarting their natural growth he is apt to destroy in them all generous vigor, replacing it by envy, destructiveness, and cruelty. There is no need for men to be cruel; on the contrary, I am persuaded that most cruelty results from thwarting in early years, above all from thwarting what is good.

Repressive and persecuting passions are very common, as the present state of the world only too amply proves. But they are not an inevitable part of human nature. On the contrary, they are, I believe, always the outcome of some kind of unhappiness. It should be one of the functions of the teacher to open vistas before his pupils showing them the possibility of activities that will be as delightful as they are useful, thereby letting loose their kind impulses and preventing the growth of a desire to rob others of joys that they will have missed. Many people decry happiness as an end, both for themselves and for others, but one may suspect them of sour grapes. It is one thing to forgo personal happiness for a public end, but it is quite another to treat the general happiness as a thing of no account. Yet this is often done in the name of some supposed heroism. In those who take this attitude there is generally some vein of cruelty based probably upon an unconscious envy, and the source of the envy will usually be found in childhood or youth. It should be the aim of the educator to train adults free from these psychological misfortunes, and not anxious to rob others of happiness because they themselves have not been robbed of it.

As matters stand today, many teachers are unable to do the best of which they are capable. For this there are a number of reasons, some more or less accidental, others very deep-seated. To begin with the former, most teachers are overworked and are compelled to prepare their pupils for examinations rather than to give them a liberalizing mental training. The people

who are not accustomed to teaching—and this includes practically all educational authorities—have no idea of the expense
of spirit that it involves. Clergymen are not expected to preach
sermons for several hours every day, but the analogous effort
is demanded of teachers. The result is that many of them become harassed and nervous, out of touch with recent work in
the subjects that they teach, and unable to inspire their students with a sense of the intellectual delights to be obtained
from new understanding and new knowledge.

This, however, is by no means the gravest matter. In most
countries certain opinions are recognized as correct, and others
as dangerous. Teachers whose opinions are not correct are expected to keep silent about them. If they mention their opinions it is propaganda, while the mentioning of correct opinions
is considered to be merely sound instruction. The result is that
the inquiring young too often have to go outside the classroom
to discover what is being thought by the most vigorous minds
of their own time. There is in America a subject called civics,
in which, perhaps more than in any other, the teaching is expected to be misleading. The young are taught a sort of copy-
book account of how public affairs are supposed to be conducted, and are carefully shielded from all knowledge as to
how in fact they are conducted. When they grow up and discover the truth, the result is too often a complete cynicism in
which all public ideals are lost; whereas if they had been
taught the truth carefully and with proper comment at an
earlier age they might have become men able to combat evils
in which, as it is, they acquiesce with a shrug.

The idea that falsehood is edifying is one of the besetting
sins of those who draw up educational schemes. I should not
myself consider that a man could be a good teacher unless he
had made a firm resolve never in the course of his teaching to
conceal truth because it is what is called "unedifying." The
kind of virtue that can be produced by guarded ignorance is

frail and fails at the first touch of reality. There are, in this world, many men who deserve admiration, and it is good that the young should be taught to see the ways in which these men are admirable. But it is not good to teach them to admire rogues by concealing their roguery. It is thought that the knowledge of things as they are will lead to cynicism, and so it may do if the knowledge comes suddenly with a shock of surprise and horror. But if it comes gradually, duly intermixed with a knowledge of what is good, and in the course of a scientific study inspired by the wish to get at the truth, it will have no such effect. In any case, to tell lies to the young, who have no means of checking what they are told, is morally indefensible.

The thing, above all, that a teacher should endeavor to produce in his pupils, if democracy is to survive, is the kind of tolerance that springs from an endeavor to understand those who are different from ourselves. It is perhaps a natural human impulse to view with horror and disgust all manners and customs different from those to which we are used. Ants and savages put strangers to death. And those who have never traveled either physically or mentally find it difficult to tolerate the queer ways and outlandish beliefs of other nations and other times, other sects and other political parties. This kind of ignorant intolerance is the antithesis of a civilized outlook, and is one of the gravest dangers to which our overcrowded world is exposed. The educational system ought to be designed to correct it, but much too little is done in this direction at present. In every country nationalistic feeling is encouraged, and school children are taught, what they are only too ready to believe, that the inhabitants of other countries are morally and intellectually inferior to those of the country in which the school children happen to reside. Collective hysteria, the most mad and cruel of all human emotions, is encouraged instead of being discouraged, and the young are encouraged to believe what they hear frequently said rather than what there is some rational ground for believing. In all this the teachers are not to blame. They are not free to teach as they would wish. It is they who know most intimately the needs of the young. It is they who through daily contact have come to care for them. But it is not they who decide what shall be taught or what the methods of instruction are to be. There ought to be a great deal more freedom than there is for the scholastic profession. It ought to have more opportunities of self-determination, more independence from the interference of bureaucrats and bigots. No one would consent in our day to subject the medical men to the control of non-medical authorities as to how they should treat their patients, except of course where they depart criminally from the purpose of medicine, which is to cure the patient. The teacher is a kind of medical man whose purpose is to cure the patient of childishness, but he is not allowed to decide for himself on the basis of experience what methods are most suitable to this end. A few great historic universities, by the weight of their prestige, have secured virtual self-determination, but the immense majority of educational institutions are hampered and controlled by men who do not understand the work with which they are interfering. The only way to prevent totalitarianism in our highly organized world is to secure a certain degree of independence for bodies performing useful public work, and among such bodies teachers deserve a foremost place.

The teacher, like the artist, the philosopher, and the man of letters, can only perform his work adequately if he feels himself to be an individual directed by an inner creative impulse, not dominated and fettered by an outside authority. It is very difficult in this modern world to find a place for the individual. He can subsist at the top as a dictator in a totalitarian state or a plutocratic magnate in a country of large industrial enterprises, but in the realm of the mind it is becoming more and more difficult to preserve independence of the great organized forces that control the livelihoods of men and women. If the world is not to lose the benefit to be derived from its best minds, it will have to find some method of allowing them scope and liberty in spite of organization. This involves a deliberate restraint on the part of those who have power, and a conscious realization that there are men to whom free scope must be afforded. Renaissance Popes could feel in this way towards Renaissance artists, but the powerful men of our day seem to have more difficulty in feeling respect for exceptional genius. The turbulence of our times is inimical to the fine flower of culture. The man in the street is full of fear, and therefore unwilling to tolerate freedoms for which he sees no need. Perhaps we must wait for quieter times before the claims of civilization can again override the claims of party spirit. Meanwhile, it is important that some at least should continue to realize the limitations of what can be done by organization. Every system should allow loopholes and exceptions, for if it does not it will in the end crush all that is best in man.

Ideas That Have Helped

Mankind

BEFORE we can discuss this subject we must form some conception as to the kind of effect that we consider a help to mankind. Are mankind helped when they become more numerous? Or when they become less like animals? Or when they become happier? Or when they learn to enjoy a greater diversity of experiences? Or when they come to know more? Or when they become more friendly to one another? I think all these things come into our conception of what helps mankind, and I will say a preliminary word about them.

The most indubitable respect in which ideas have helped mankind is numbers. There must have been a time when *homo sapiens* was a very rare species, subsisting precariously in jungles and caves, terrified of wild beasts, having difficulty in securing nourishment. At this period the biological advantage of his greater intelligence, which was cumulative because it could be handed on from generation to generation, had scarcely begun to outweigh the disadvantages of his long infancy, his lessened agility as compared with monkeys, and his lack of hirsute protection against cold. In those days, the number of men must certainly have been very small. The main use to which, throughout the ages, men have put their technical skill has been to increase the total population. I do not mean that this was the intention, but that it was, in fact, the effect. If this is something to rejoice in, then we have occasion to rejoice.

We have also become, in certain respects, progressively less like animals. I can think in particular of two respects: first, that acquired, as opposed to congenital, skills play a continually increasing part in human life, and, secondly, that forethought more and more dominates impulse. In these respects we have certainly become progressively less like animals.

As to happiness, I am not so sure. Birds, it is true, die of hunger in large numbers during the winter, if they are not birds of passage. But during the summer they do not foresee this catastrophe, or remember how nearly it befell them in the previous winter. With human beings the matter is otherwise. I doubt whether the percentage of birds that will have died of hunger during the present winter (1946–7) is as great as the percentage of human beings that will have died from this cause in India and Central Europe during the same period. But every human death by starvation is preceded by a long period of anxiety, and surrounded by the corresponding anxiety of neighbors. We suffer not only the evils that actually befall us, but all those that our intelligence tells us we have reason to fear. The curbing of impulses to which we are led by forethought averts physical disaster at the cost of worry, and general lack of joy. I do not think that the learned men of my acquaintance, even when they enjoy a secure income, are as happy as the mice that eat the crumbs from their tables while the erudite gentlemen snooze. In this respect, therefore, I am not convinced that there has been any progress at all.

As to diversity of enjoyments, however, the matter is otherwise. I remember reading an account of some lions who were taken to a movie showing the successful depredations of lions in a wild state, but none of them got any pleasure from the spectacle. Not only music, and poetry, and science, but football, and baseball, and alcohol, afford no pleasure to animals. Our intelligence has, therefore, certainly enabled us to get a much greater variety of enjoyment than is open to animals, but we have purchased this advantage at the expense of a much greater liability to boredom.

But I shall be told that it is neither numbers nor multiplicity of pleasures that make the glory of man. It is his intellectual and moral qualities. It is obvious that we know more than animals do, and it is common to consider this one of our advantages. Whether it is, in fact, an advantage, may be doubted. But at any rate it is something that distinguishes us from the brutes.

Has civilization taught us to be more friendly towards one another? The answer is easy. Robins (the English, not the American species) peck an elderly robin to death, whereas men (the English, not the American species) give an elderly man an old-age pension. Within the herd we are more friendly to each other than are many species of animals, but in our attitude towards those outside the herd, in spite of all that has been done by moralists and religious teachers, our emotions are as ferocious as those of any animal, and our intelligence enables us to give them a scope which is denied to even the most savage beast. It may be hoped, though not very confidently, that the more humane attitude will in time come to prevail, but so far the omens are not very propitious.

All these different elements must be borne in mind in considering what ideas have done most to help mankind. The ideas with which we shall be concerned may be broadly divided into two kinds: those that contribute to knowledge and technique, and those that are concerned with morals and politics.

I will treat first those that have to do with knowledge and technique.

The most important and difficult steps were taken before the dawn of history. At what stage language began is not known, but we may be pretty certain that it began very gradually. Without it it would have been very difficult to hand on from generation to generation the inventions and discoveries that were gradually made.

Another great step, which may have come either before or after the beginning of language, was the utilization of fire. I suppose that at first fire was chiefly used to keep away wild beasts while our ancestors slept, but the warmth must have been found agreeable. Presumably on some occasion a child got scolded for throwing the meat into the fire, but when it was taken out it was found to be much better, and so the long history of cookery began.

The taming of domestic animals, especially the cow and the sheep, must have made life much pleasanter and more secure. Some anthropologists have an attractive theory that the utility of domestic animals was not foreseen, but that people attempted to tame whatever animal their religion taught them to worship. The tribes that worshiped lions and crocodiles died out, while those to whom the cow or the sheep was a sacred animal prospered. I like this theory, and in the entire absence of evidence, for or against it, I feel at liberty to play with it.

Even more important than the domestication of animals was the invention of agriculture, which, however, introduced bloodthirsty practices into religion that lasted for many centuries. Fertility rites tended to involve human sacrifice and cannibalism. Moloch would not help the corn to grow unless he was allowed to feast on the blood of children. A similar opinion was adopted by the Evangelicals of Manchester in the early days of industrialism, when they kept six-year-old chil-

dren working twelve to fourteen hours a day, in conditions
that caused most of them to die. It has now been discovered
that grain will grow, and cotton goods can be manufactured,
without being watered by the blood of infants. In the case of
the grain, the discovery took thousands of years; in the case
of the cotton goods hardly a century. So perhaps there is some
evidence of progress in the world.

The last of the great prehistoric inventions was the art of
writing, which was indeed a prerequisite of history. Writing,
like speech, developed gradually, and in the form of pictures
designed to convey a message it was probably as old as speech,
but from pictures to syllable writing and thence to the alphabet
was a very slow evolution. In China the last step was never
taken.

Coming to historic times, we find that the earliest important
steps were taken in mathematics and astronomy, both of which
began in Babylonia some millennia before the beginning of our
era. Learning in Babylonia seems, however, to have become
stereotyped and non-progressive, long before the Greeks first
came into contact with it. It is to the Greeks that we owe ways
of thinking and investigating that have ever since been found
fruitful. In the prosperous Greek commercial cities, rich men
living on slave labor were brought by the processes of trade
into contact with many nations, some quite barbarous, others
fairly civilized. What the civilized nations—the Babylonians
and Egyptians—had to offer the Greeks quickly assimilated.
They became critical of their own traditional customs, by per-
ceiving them to be at once analogous to, and different from,
the customs of surrounding inferior peoples, and so by the
sixth century B.C. some of them achieved a degree of enlightened rationalism which cannot be surpassed in the present day.
Xenophanes observed that men make gods in their own image
—"the Ethiopians make their gods black and snub-nosed; the
Thracians say theirs have blue eyes and red hair: Yes, and if

oxen and lions and horses had hands, and could paint with their hands, and produced works of art as men do, horses would paint the forms of gods like horses, and oxen like oxen, and make their bodies in the image of their several kinds."

Some Greeks used their emancipation from tradition in the pursuit of mathematics and astronomy, in both of which they made the most amazing progress. Mathematics was not used by the Greeks, as it is by the moderns, to facilitate industrial processes; it was a "gentlemanly" pursuit, valued for its own sake as giving eternal truth, and a supersensible standard by which the visible world was condemned as second-rate. Only Archimedes foreshadowed the modern use of mathematics by inventing engines of war for the defense of Syracuse against the Romans. A Roman soldier killed him and the mathematicians retired again into their ivory tower.

Astronomy, which the sixteenth and seventeenth centuries pursued with ardor, largely because of its usefulness in navigation, was pursued by the Greeks with no regard for practical utility, except when, in later antiquity, it became associated with astrology. At a very early stage they discovered the earth to be round and made a fairly accurate estimate of its size. They discovered ways of calculating the distance of the sun and moon, and Aristarchus of Samos even evolved the complete Copernican hypothesis, but his views were rejected by all his followers except one, and after the third century B.C. no very important progress was made. At the time of the Renaissance, however, something of what the Greeks had done became known, and greatly facilitated the rise of modern science.

The Greeks had the conception of natural law, and acquired the habit of expressing natural laws in mathematical terms. These ideas have provided the key to a very great deal of the understanding of the physical world that has been achieved in modern times. But many of them, including Aristotle, were misled by a belief that science could make a fruitful use of the idea of purpose. Aristotle distinguished four kinds of cause, of which only two concern us, the "efficient" cause and the "final" cause. The "efficient" cause is what *we* should call simply the cause. The "final" cause is the purpose. For instance, if, in the course of a tramp in the mountains, you find an inn just when your thirst has become unendurable, the efficient cause of the inn is the actions of the bricklayers that built it, while its final cause is the satisfaction of your thirst. If someone were to ask "why is there an inn there?" it would be equally appropriate to answer "because someone had it built there" or "because many thirsty travelers pass that way." One is an explanation by the "efficient" cause and the other by the "final" cause. Where human affairs are concerned, the explanation by "final" cause is often appropriate, since human actions have purposes. But where inanimate nature is concerned, only "efficient" causes have been found scientifically discoverable, and the attempt to explain phenomena by "final" causes has always led to bad science. There may, for aught we know, be a purpose in natural phenomena, but if so it has remained completely undiscovered, and all known scientific laws have to do only with "efficient" causes. In this respect Aristotle led the world astray, and it did not recover fully until the time of Galileo.

The seventeenth century, especially Galileo, Descartes, Newton, and Leibniz, made an advance in our understanding of nature more sudden and surprising than any other in history, except that of the early Greeks. It is true that some of the concepts used in the mathematical physics of that time had not quite the validity that was then ascribed to them. It is true also that the more recent advances of physics often require new concepts quite different from those of the seventeenth century. Their concepts, in fact, were not the key to *all* the secrets of nature, but they were the key to a great many. Modern technique in industry and war, with the sole exception of the atomic bomb, is still wholly based upon a type of dynamics developed out of the principles of Galileo and Newton. Most of astronomy still rests upon these same principles, though there are some problems such as "what keeps the sun hot?" in which the recent discoveries of quantum mechanics are essential. The dynamics of Galileo and Newton depended upon two new principles and a new technique.

The first of the new principles was the law of inertia, which stated that any body, left to itself, will continue to move as it is moving in the same straight line, and with the same velocity. The importance of this principle is only evident when it is contrasted with the principles that the scholastics had evolved out of Aristotle. Before Galileo it was held that there was a radical difference between regions below the moon and regions from the moon upwards. In the regions below the moon, the "sublunary" sphere, there was change and decay; the "natural" motion of bodies was rectilinear, but any body in motion, if left to itself, would gradually slow up and presently stop. From the moon upwards, on the contrary, the "natural" motion of bodies was circular, or compounded of circular motions, and in the heavens there was no such thing as change or decay, except the periodic changes of the orbits of the heavenly bodies. The movements of the heavenly bodies were not spontaneous, but were passed on to them from the *primum mobile*, which was the outermost of the moving spheres, and itself derived its motion from the Unmoved Mover, i.e. God. No one thought of making any appeal to observation; for instance, it was held that a projectile will first move horizontally for a while, and then suddenly begin to fall vertically, although it might have been supposed that anybody watching a fountain could have seen that the drops move in curves. Comets, since they appear and disappear, had to be supposed to be between the earth and the moon, for if they had been above the moon they would have had to be indestructible. It is evident that out of such a jumble nothing could be developed. Galileo unified the principles of governing the earth and the heavens by his single law of inertia, according to which a body, once in motion, will not stop of itself, but will move with a constant velocity in a straight line whether it is on earth or in one of the celestial spheres. This principle made it possible to develop a science of the motions of matter, without taking account of any supposed influence of mind or spirit, and thus laid the foundations of the purely materialistic physics in which men of science, however pious, have ever since believed.

From the seventeenth century onwards, it has become increasingly evident that if we wish to understand natural laws, we must get rid of every kind of ethical and aesthetic bias. We must cease to think that noble things have noble causes, that intelligent things have intelligent causes, or that order is impossible without a celestial policeman. The Greeks admired the sun and moon and planets, and supposed them to be gods; Plotinus explains how superior they are to human beings in wisdom and virtue. Anaxagoras, who taught otherwise, was prosecuted for impiety and compelled to fly from Athens. The Greeks also allowed themselves to think that since the circle is the most perfect figure, the motions of the heavenly bodies must be, or be derived from, circular motions. Every bias of this sort had to be discarded by seventeenth-century astronomy. The Copernican system showed that the earth is not the center of the universe, and suggested to a few bold spirits that perhaps man was not the supreme purpose of the Creator. In the main, however, astronomers were pious folk, and until the nineteenth century most of them, except in France, believed in Genesis.

It was geology, Darwin, and the doctrine of evolution, that first upset the faith of British men of science. If man was evolved by insensible gradations from lower forms of life, a number of things became very difficult to understand. At what moment in evolution did our ancestors acquire free will? At what stage in the long journey from the amoeba did they begin to have immortal souls? When did they first become capable of the kinds of wickedness that would justify a benevolent Creator in sending them into eternal torment? Most people felt that such punishment would be hard on monkeys, in spite of their propensity for throwing coconuts at the heads of Europeans. But how about *Pithecanthropus Erectus?* Was it really he who ate the apple? Or was it *Homo Pekiniensis?* Or was it perhaps the Piltdown man? I went to Piltdown once, but saw no evidence of special depravity in that village, nor did I see any signs of its having changed appreciably since prehistoric ages. Perhaps then it was the Neanderthal men who first sinned? This seems the more likely, as they lived in Germany. But obviously there can be no answer to such questions, and those theologians who do not wholly reject evolution have had to make profound readjustments.

One of the "grand" conceptions which have proved scientifically useless is the soul. I do not mean that there is positive evidence showing that men have no souls; I only mean that the soul, if it exists, plays no part in any discoverable causal law. There are all kinds of experimental methods of determining how men and animals behave under various circumstances. You can put rats in mazes and men in barbed wire cages, and observe their methods of escape. You can administer drugs and observe their effect. You can turn a male rat into a female, though so far nothing analogous has been done with human beings, even at Buchenwald. It appears that socially undesirable conduct can be dealt with by medical means, or by creating a better environment, and the conception of sin has thus come to seem quite unscientific, except, of course, as applied to the Nazis. There is real hope that, by getting to understand the science of human behavior, governments may

be even more able than they are at present to turn mankind
into rabbles of mutually ferocious lunatics. Governments could,
of course, do exactly the opposite and cause the human race
to co-operate willingly and cheerfully in making themselves
happy, rather than in making others miserable, but only if
there is an international government with a monopoly of
armed force. It is very doubtful whether this will take place.

This brings me to the second kind of idea that has helped
or may in time help mankind; I mean moral as opposed to
technical ideas. Hitherto I have been considering the increased
command over the forces of nature which men have derived
from scientific knowledge, but this, although it is a pre-condi-
tion of many forms of progress, does not of itself insure anything desirable. On the contrary, the present state of the world
and the fear of an atomic war show that scientific progress
without a corresponding moral and political progress may
only increase the magnitude of the disaster that misdirected
skill may bring about. In superstitious moments I am
tempted to believe in the myth of the Tower of Babel, and to
suppose that in our own day a similar but greater impiety is
about to be visited by a more tragic and terrible punishment.
Perhaps—so I sometimes allow myself to fancy—God does
not intend us to understand the mechanism by which He
regulates the material universe. Perhaps the nuclear physicists
have come so near to the ultimate secrets that He thinks it
time to bring their activities to a stop. And what simpler
method could He devise than to let them carry their ingenuity
to the point where they exterminate the human race? If I could
think that deer and squirrels, nightingales and larks, would
survive, I might view this catastrophe with some equanimity,
since man has not shown himself worthy to be the lord of creation. But it is to be feared that the dreadful alchemy of the
atomic bomb will destroy all forms of life equally, and that
the earth will remain forever a dead clod senselessly whirling

round a futile sun. I do not know the immediate precipitating cause of this interesting occurrence. Perhaps it will be a dispute about Persian oil, perhaps a disagreement as to Chinese trade, perhaps a quarrel between Jews and Mohommedans for the control of Palestine. Any patriotic person can see that these issues are of such importance as to make the extermination of mankind preferable to cowardly conciliation.

In case, however, there should be some among my readers who would like to see the human race survive, it may be worth while considering the stock of moral ideas that great men have put into the world and that might, if they were listened to, secure happiness instead of misery for the mass of mankind.

Man, viewed morally, is a strange amalgam of angel and devil. He can feel the splendor of the night, the delicate beauty of spring flowers, the tender emotion of parental love, and the intoxication of intellectual understanding. In moments of insight visions come to him of how life should be lived and how men should order their dealings one with another. Universal love is an emotion which many have felt and which many more could feel if the world made it less difficult. This is one side of the picture. On the other side are cruelty, greed, indifference and overweening pride. Men, quite ordinary men, will compel children to look on while their mothers are raped. In pursuit of political aims men will submit their opponents to long years of unspeakable anguish. We know what the Nazis did to Jews at Auschwitz. In mass cruelty, the expulsions of Germans ordered by the Russians fall not very far short of the atrocities perpetuated by the Nazis. And how about our noble selves? We would not do such deeds, oh no! But we enjoy our juicy steaks and our hot rolls while German children die of hunger because our governments dare not face our indignation if they asked us to forgo some part of our pleasures. If there were a Last Judgment as Christians believe, how do you think our excuses would sound before that final tribunal?

Moral ideas sometimes wait upon political developments, and sometimes outrun them. The brotherhood of man is an ideal which owed its first force to political developments. When Alexander conquered the East he set to work to obliterate the distinction of Greek and barbarian, no doubt because his Greek and Macedonian army was too small to hold down so vast an empire by force. He compelled his officers to marry barbarian aristocratic ladies, while he himself, to set a doubly excellent example, married *two* barbarian princesses. As a result of this policy Greek pride and exclusiveness were diminished, and Greek culture spread to many regions not inhabited by Hellenic stock. Zeno, the founder of Stoicism, who was probably a boy at the time of Alexander's conquest, was a Phoenician, and few of the eminent Stoics were Greeks. It was the Stoics who invented the conception of the brotherhood of man. They taught that all men are children of Zeus and that the sage will ignore the distinctions of Greek and barbarian, bond and free. When Rome brought the whole civilized world under one government, the political environment was favorable to the spread of this doctrine. In a new form, more capable of appealing to the emotions of ordinary men and women, Christianity taught a similar doctrine. Christ said "Thou shalt love thy neighbor as thyself," and when asked "who is thy neighbor?" went on to the parable of the Good Samaritan. If you wish to understand this parable as it was understood by his hearers, you should substitute "German" or "Japanese" for "Samaritan." I fear many present-day Christians would resent such a substitution, because it would compel them to realize how far they have departed from the teaching of the Founder of their religion. A similar doctrine had been taught much earlier by the Buddhists. According to them, the Buddha declared that he could not be happy so long as even one man remained miserable. It might seem as if these lofty ethical teachings had little effect upon the world; in

India Buddhism died out, in Europe Christianity was emptied of most of the elements it derived from Christ. But I think this would be a superficial view. Christianity, as soon as it conquered the state, put an end to gladiatorial shows, not because they were cruel, but because they were idolatrous. The result, however, was to diminish the widespread education in cruelty by which the populace of Roman towns were degraded. Christianity also did much to soften the lot of slaves. It established charity on a large scale, and inaugurated hospitals. Although the great majority of Christians failed lamentably in Christian charity, the ideal remained alive and in every age inspired some notable saints. In a new form, it passed over into modern Liberalism, and remains the inspiration of much that is most hopeful in our somber world.

The watchwords of the French Revolution, Liberty, Equality, and Fraternity, have religious origins. Of Fraternity I have already spoken. Equality was a characteristic of the Orphic Societies in ancient Greece, from which, indirectly, a great deal of Christian dogma took its rise. In these Societies, slaves and women were admitted on equal terms with citizens. Plato's advocacy of Votes for Women, which has seemed surprising to some modern readers, is derived from Orphic practices. The Orphics believed in transmigration and thought that a soul which in one life inhabits the body of a slave, may, in another, inhabit that of a king. Viewed from the standpoint of religion, it is therefore foolish to discriminate between a slave and a king; both share the dignity belonging to an immortal soul, and neither, in religion, can claim anything more. This point of view passed over from Orphism into Stoicism, and into Christianity. For a long time its practical effect was small, but ultimately, whenever circumstances were favorable, it helped in bringing about the diminution of the inequalities in the social system. Read, for instance, John Woolman's Journal. John Woolman was a Quaker, one of the first Americans to oppose slavery. No doubt the real ground of his opposition was humane feeling, but he was able to fortify this feeling and to make it controversially more effective by appeals to Christian doctrines, which his neighbors did not dare to repudiate openly.

Liberty as an ideal has had a very checkered history. In antiquity, Sparta, which was a totalitarian state, had as little use for it as the Nazis had. But most of the Greek city states allowed a degree of liberty which we should now think excessive, and, in fact, do think excessive when it is practiced by their descendants in the same part of the world. Politics was a matter of assassination and rival armies, one of them supporting the government, and the other composed of refugees. The refugees would often ally themselves with their city's enemies and march in in triumph on the heels of foreign conquerors. This sort of thing was done by everybody, and, in spite of much fine talk in the works of modern historians about Greek loyalty to the city state, nobody seemed to view such conduct as particularly nefarious. This was carrying liberty to excess, and led by reaction to admiration of Sparta.

The word "liberty" has had strange meanings at different times. In Rome, in the last days of the Republic and the early days of the Empire, it meant the right of powerful Senators to plunder Provinces for their private profit. Brutus, whom most English-speaking readers know as the high-minded hero of Shakespeare's *Julius Caesar*, was, in fact, rather different from this. He would lend money to a municipality at 60 per cent, and when they failed to pay the interest he would hire a private army to besiege them, for which his friend Cicero mildly expostulated with him. In our own day, the word "liberty" bears a very similar meaning when used by industrial magnates. Leaving these vagaries on one side, there are two serious meanings of the word "liberty." On the one hand the freedom of a nation from foreign domination, on the other hand, the freedom of the citizen to pursue his legitimate avocations. Each of these in a well-ordered world should be subject to limitations, but unfortunately the former has been taken in an absolute sense. To this point of view I will return presently; it is the liberty of the individual citizen that I now wish to speak about.

This kind of liberty first entered practical politics in the form of religious toleration, a doctrine which came to be widely adopted in the seventeenth century through the inability of either Protestants or Catholics to exterminate the opposite party. After they had fought each other for a hundred years, culminating in the horror of the thirty years' war, and after it had appeared that as a result of all this bloodshed the balance of parties at the end was almost exactly what it had been at the beginning, certain men of genius, mostly Dutchmen, suggested that perhaps all the killing had been unnecessary, and that people might be allowed to think what they chose on such matters as consubstantiation versus transubstantiation, or whether the Cup should be allowed to the laity. The doctrine of religious toleration came to England with the Dutch King William, along with the Bank of England and the National Debt. In fact all three were products of the commercial mentality.

The greatest of the theoretical advocates of liberty at that period was John Locke, who devoted much thought to the problem of reconciling the maximum of liberty with the indispensable minimum of government, a problem with which his successors in the Liberal tradition have been occupied down to the present day.

In addition to religious freedom, free press, free speech, and freedom from arbitrary arrest came to be taken for granted during the nineteenth century, at least among the Western democracies. But their hold on men's minds was much more precarious than was at the time supposed, and now, over the greater part of the earth's surface, nothing remains of them, either in practice or in theory. Stalin could neither understand nor respect the point of view which led Churchill to allow himself to be peaceably dispossessed as a result of a popular vote. I am a firm believer in democratic representative government as the best form for those who have the tolerance and self-restraint that is required to make it workable. But its advocates make a mistake if they suppose that it can be at once introduced into countries where the average citizen has hitherto lacked all training in the give-and-take that it requires. In a Balkan country, not so many years ago, a party which had been beaten by a narrow margin in a general election retrieved its fortunes by shooting a sufficient number of the representatives of the other side to give it a majority. People in the West thought this characteristic of the Balkans, forgetting that Cromwell and Robespierre had acted likewise.

And this brings me to the last pair of great political ideas to which mankind owes whatever little success in social organization it has achieved. I mean the ideas of law and government. Of these, government is the more fundamental. Government can easily exist without law, but law cannot exist without government—a fact which was forgotten by those who framed the League of Nations and the Kellogg Pact. Government may be defined as a concentration of the collective forces of a community in a certain organization which, in virtue of this concentration, is able to control individual citizens and to resist pressure from foreign states. War has always been the chief promoter of governmental power. The control of government over the private citizen is always greater where there is war or imminent danger of war than where peace seems secure. But when governments have acquired power with a view to resisting foreign aggression, they have naturally used it, if they could, to further their private interests at the expense of the citizens. Absolute monarchy was, until recently, the grossest form of this abuse of power. But in the modern totalitarian state the same evil has been carried much further than had been dreamed of by Xerxes or Nero or any of the tyrants of earlier times.

Democracy was invented as a device for reconciling government with liberty. It is clear that government is necessary if anything worthy to be called civilization is to exist, but all history shows that any set of men entrusted with power over another set will abuse their power if they can do so with impunity. Democracy is intended to make men's tenure of power temporary and dependent upon popular approval. In so far as it achieves this it prevents the worst abuses of power. The Second Triumvirate in Rome, when they wanted money with a view to fighting Brutus and Cassius, made a list of rich men and declared them public enemies, cut off their heads, and seized their property. This sort of procedure is not possible in America and England at the present day. We owe the fact that it is not possible not only to democracy, but also to the doctrine of personal liberty. This doctrine, in practice, consists of two parts, on the one hand that a man shall not be punished except by due process of law, and on the other hand that there shall be a sphere within which a man's actions are not to be subject to governmental control. This sphere includes free speech, free press and religious freedom. It used to include freedom of economic enterprise. All these doctrines, of course, are held in practice with certain limitations. The British formerly did not adhere to them in their dealings with India. Freedom of the press is not respected in the case of doctrines which are thought dangerously subversive. Free speech would not be held to exonerate public advocacy of assassination of an unpopular politician. But in spite of these limitations the doctrine of personal liberty has been of great value throughout the English-speaking world, as anyone who lives in it will quickly realize when he finds himself in a police state.

In the history of social evolution it will be found that almost invariably the establishment of some sort of government has come first and attempts to make government compatible with personal liberty have come later. In international affairs we have not yet reached the first stage, although it is now evident that international government is at least as important to mankind as national government. I think it may be seriously doubted whether the next twenty years would be more disastrous to mankind if all government were abolished than they will be if no effective international government is established. I find it often urged that an international government would be oppressive, and I do not deny that this might be the case, at any rate for a time, but national governments were oppressive when they were new and are still oppressive in most countries, and yet hardly anybody would on this ground advocate anarchy within a nation.

Ordered social life of a kind that could seem in any degree desirable rests upon a synthesis and balance of certain slowly developed ideas and institutions: government, law, individual liberty, and democracy. Individual liberty, of course, existed in the ages before there was government, but when it existed without government civilized life was impossible. When governments first arose they involved slavery, absolute monarchy, and usually the enforcement of superstitition by a powerful priesthood. All these were very great evils, and one can understand Rousseau's nostalgia for the life of the noble savage. But this was a mere romantic idealization, and, in fact, the life of the savage was, as Hobbes said, "nasty, brutish, and short." The history of man reaches occasional great crises. There must have been a crisis when the apes lost their tails, and another when our ancestors took to walking upright and lost their protective covering of hair. As I remarked before, the human population of the globe, which must at one time have been very small, was greatly increased by the invention of agriculture, and was in-

creased again in our own time by modern industrial and medical technique. But modern technique has brought us to a new
crisis. In this new crisis we are faced with an alternative: either
man must again become a rare species as in the days of *Homo
Pekiniensis*, or we must learn to submit to an international
government. Any such government, whether good, bad or indifferent, will make the continuation of the human species
possible, and, as in the course of the past 5,000 years men have
climbed gradually from the despotism of the Pharaohs to the
glories of the American Constitution, so perhaps in the next
5,000 they may climb from a bad international government to
a good one. But if they do not establish an international government of some kind, new progress will have to begin at a
lower level, probably at that of tribal savagery, and will have
to begin after a cataclysmic destruction only to be paralleled
by the Biblical account of the deluge. When we survey the
long development of mankind from a rare hunted animal, hid-
ing precariously in caves from the fury of wild beasts which
he was incapable of killing; subsisting doubtfully on the raw
fruits of the earth which he did not know how to cultivate;
reinforcing real terrors by the imaginary terrors of ghosts and
evil spirits and malign spells; gradually acquiring the mastery
of his environment by the invention of fire, writing, weapons,
and at last science; building up a social organization which
curbed private violence and gave a measure of security to daily
life; using the leisure gained by his skill, not only in idle luxury,
but in the production of beauty and the unveiling of the
secrets of natural law; learning gradually, though imperfectly,
to view an increasing number of his neighbors as allies in the
task of production rather than enemies in the attempts at mutual depredation—when we consider this long and arduous
journey, it becomes intolerable to think that it may all have
to be made again from the beginning owing to failure to take
one step for which past developments, rightly viewed, have

been a preparation. Social cohesion, which among the apes is confined to the family, grew in prehistoric times as far as the tribe, and in the very beginnings of history reached the level of small kingdoms in upper and lower Egypt and in Mesopotamia. From these small kingdoms grew the empires of antiquity, and then gradually the great states of our own day, far larger than even the Roman Empire. Quite recent developments have robbed the smaller states of any real independence, until now there remain only two that are wholly capable of independent self-direction: I mean, of course, the United States and the U.S.S.R. All that is necessary to save mankind from disaster is the step from two independent states to one— not by war, which would bring disaster, but by agreement.

If this step can be accomplished, all the great achievements of mankind will quickly lead to an era of happiness and well-being, such as has never before been dreamed of. Our scientific skill will make it possible to abolish poverty throughout the world without necessitating more than four or five hours a day of productive labor. Disease, which has been very rapidly reduced during the last hundred years, will be reduced still further. The leisure achieved through organization and science will no doubt be devoted very largely to pure enjoyment, but there will remain a number of people to whom the pursuit of art and science will seem important. There will be a new freedom from economic bondage to the mere necessities of keeping alive, and the great mass of mankind may enjoy the kind of carefree adventurousness that characterizes the rich young Athenians of Plato's Dialogues. All this is easily within the bounds of technical possibility. It requires for its realization only one thing: that the men who hold power, and the populations that support them, should think it more important to keep themselves alive than to cause the death of their enemies. No very lofty or difficult ideal, one might think, and yet one which so far has proved beyond the scope of human intelligence.

The present moment is the most important and most crucial that has ever confronted mankind. Upon our collective wisdom during the next twenty years depends the question whether mankind shall be plunged into unparalleled disaster, or shall achieve a new level of happiness, security, well-being, and intelligence. I do not know which mankind will choose. There is grave reason for fear, but there is enough possibility of a good solution to make hope not irrational. And it is on this hope that we must act.

X

Ideas That Have Harmed Mankind

THE misfortunes of human beings may be divided into two classes: First, those inflicted by the nonhuman environment, and, second, those inflicted by other people. As mankind have progressed in knowledge and technique, the second class has become a continually increasing percentage of the total. In old times, famine, for example, was due to natural causes, and, although people did their best to combat it, large numbers of them died of starvation. At the present moment large parts of the world are faced with the threat of famine, but although natural causes have contributed to the situation, the principal causes are human. For six years the civilized nations of the world devoted all their best energies to killing each other, and they find it difficult suddenly to switch over to keeping each other alive. Having destroyed harvests, dismantled agricultural machinery, and disorganized shipping, they find it no easy matter to relieve the shortage of crops in one place by means of a superabundance in another, as would easily be done if the economic system were in normal working order. As this illustration shows, it is now man that is man's worst enemy. Nature, it is true, still sees to it that we are mortal, but with the progress in medicine it will become more and more common for people to live until they have had their fill of life. We are supposed to wish to live forever and to look forward to the unending joys of heaven, of which, by miracle, the monotony will never grow stale. But in fact, if you question any candid person who is no longer young, he is very likely to tell you that, having tasted life in this world, he has no wish to begin again as a "new boy" in another. For the future, therefore, it may be taken that much the most important evils that mankind have to consider are those which they inflict upon each other through stupidity or malevolence or both.

I think that the evils that men inflict on each other, and by reflection upon themselves, have their main source in evil passions rather than in ideas or beliefs. But ideas and principles that do harm are, as a rule, though not always, cloaks for evil passions. In Lisbon when heretics were publicly burned, it sometimes happened that one of them, by a particularly edifying recantation, would be granted the boon of being strangled before being put into the flames. This would make the spectators so furious that the authorities had great difficulty in preventing them from lynching the penitent and burning him on their own account. The spectacle of the writhing torments of the victims was, in fact, one of the principal pleasures to which the populace looked forward to enliven a somewhat drab existence. I cannot doubt that this pleasure greatly contributed to the general belief that the burning of heretics was a righteous act. The same sort of thing applies to war. People who are vigorous and brutal often find war enjoyable, provided that it is a victorious war and that there is not too much interference with rape and plunder. This is a great help in persuading people that wars are righteous. Dr. Arnold, the hero of *Tom Brown's Schooldays*, and the admired reformer of public schools, came across some cranks who thought it a mistake to flog boys. Anyone reading his outburst of furious indignation against this opinion will be forced to the conclusion that he enjoyed inflicting floggings, and did not wish to be deprived of this pleasure.

It would be easy to multiply instances in support of the thesis that opinions which justify cruelty are inspired by cruel impulses. When we pass in review the opinions of former times which are now recognized as absurd, it will be found that nine times out of ten they were such as to justify the infliction of suffering. Take, for instance, medical practice. When anaesthetics were invented they were thought to be wicked as being an attempt to thwart God's will. Insanity was thought to be due to diabolic possession, and it was believed that demons inhabiting a madman could be driven out by inflicting pain upon him, and so making them uncomfortable. In pursuit of this opinion, lunatics were treated for years on end with systematic and conscientious brutality. I cannot think of any instance of an erroneous medical treatment that was agreeable rather than disagreeable to the patient. Or again, take moral education. Consider how much brutality has been justified by the rhyme:

> A dog, a wife, and a walnut tree,
> The more you beat them the better they be.

I have no experience of the moral effect of flagellation on walnut trees, but no civilized person would now justify the rhyme as regards wives. The reformative effect of punishment is a belief that dies hard, chiefly I think, because it is so satisfying to our sadistic impulses.

But although passions have had more to do than beliefs with what is amiss in human life, yet beliefs, especially where they are ancient and systematic and embodied in organizations, have a great power of delaying desirable changes of opinion and of influencing in the wrong direction people who otherwise would have no strong feelings either way. Since my subject is *"Ideas That Have Harmed Mankind,"* it is especially harmful systems of beliefs that I shall consider.

The most obvious case as regards past history is constituted by the beliefs which may be called religious or superstitious, according to one's personal bias. It was supposed that human sacrifice would improve the crops, at first for purely magical reasons, and then because the blood of victims was thought pleasing to the gods, who certainly were made in the image of their worshipers. We read in the Old Testament that it was a religious duty to exterminate conquered races completely, and that to spare even their cattle and sheep was an impiety. Dark terrors and misfortunes in the life to come oppressed the Egyptians and Etruscans, but never reached their full development until the victory of Christianity. Gloomy saints who abstained from all pleasures of sense, who lived in solitude in the desert, denying themselves meat and wine and the society of women, were, nevertheless, not obliged to abstain from *all* pleasures. The pleasures of the mind were considered to be superior to those of the body, and a high place among the pleasures of the mind was assigned to the contemplation of the eternal tortures to which the pagans and heretics would hereafter be subjected. It is one of the drawbacks to asceticism that it sees no harm in pleasures other than those of sense, and yet, in fact, not only the best pleasures, but also the very worst, are purely mental. Consider the pleasures of Milton's Satan when he contemplates the harm that he could do to man. As Milton makes him say:

> The mind is its own place, and of itself
> Can make a hell of heaven, a heaven of hell.

and his psychology is not so very different from that of Tertullian, exulting in the thought that he will be able to look out from heaven at the sufferings of the damned. The ascetic depreciation of the pleasures of sense has not promoted kindliness or tolerance, or any of the other virtues that a non-superstitious outlook on human life would lead us to desire. On the contrary, when a man tortures himself he feels that it gives him a right to torture others, and inclines him to accept any system of dogma by which this right is fortified.

The ascetic form of cruelty is, unfortunately, not confined to the fiercer forms of Christian dogma, which are now seldom believed with their former ferocity. The world has produced new and menacing forms of the same psychological pattern. The Nazis in the days before they achieved power lived laborious lives, involving much sacrifice of ease and present pleasure in obedience to the belief in strenuousness and Nietzsche's maxim that one should make oneself hard. Even after they achieved power, the slogan "guns rather than butter" still involved a sacrifice of the pleasures of sense for the mental pleasures of prospective victory—the very pleasures, in fact, with which Milton's Satan consoles himself while tortured by the fires of hell. The same mentality is to be found among earnest Communists, to whom luxury is an evil, hard work the principal duty, and universal poverty the means to the millennium. The combination of asceticism and cruelty has not disappeared with the softening of Christian dogma, but has taken on new forms hostile to Christianity. There is still much of the same mentality: mankind are divided into saints and sinners; the saints are to achieve bliss in the Nazi or Communist heaven, while the sinners are to be liquidated, or to suffer such pains as human beings can inflict in concentration camps—inferior, of course, to those which Omnipotence was thought to inflict in hell, but the worst that human beings with their limited powers are able to achieve. There is still, for the saints, a hard period of probation followed by "the shout of them that triumph, the song of them that feast," as the Christian hymn says in describing the joys of heaven.

As this psychological pattern seems so persistent and so capable of clothing itself in completely new mantles of dogma, it must have its roots somewhat deep in human nature. This is the kind of matter that is studied by psychoanalysts, and while I am very far from subscribing to all their doctrines, I think that their general methods are important if we wish to seek out the source of evil in our innermost depths. The twin conceptions of sin and vindictive punishment seem to be at the root of much that is most vigorous, both in religion and politics. I cannot believe, as some psychoanalysts do, that the feeling of sin is innate, though I believe it to be a product of very early infancy. I think that, if this feeling could be eradicated, the amount of cruelty in the world would be very greatly diminished. Given that we are all sinners and that we all deserve punishment, there is evidently much to be said for a system that causes the punishment to fall upon others than ourselves. Calvinists, by the fiat of undeserved mercy, would go to heaven, and their feelings that sin deserved punishment would receive a merely vicarious satisfaction. Communists have a similar outlook. When we are born we do not choose whether we are to be born capitalists or proletarians, but if the latter we are among the elect, and if the former we are not. Without any choice on our own parts, by the working of economic determinism, we are fated to be on the right side in the one case, and on the wrong side in the other. Marx's father became a Christian when Marx was a little boy, and some, at least, of the dogmas he must have then accepted seem to have borne fruit in his son's psychology.

One of the odd effects of the importance which each of us attaches to himself is that we tend to imagine our own good or evil fortune to be the purpose of other people's actions. If you pass in a train a field containing grazing cows, you may sometimes see them running away in terror as the train passes. The cow, if it were a metaphysician, would argue: "Everything in my own desires and hopes and fears has reference to myself; hence by induction I conclude that everything in the universe has reference to myself. This noisy train, therefore, intends to do me either good or evil. I cannot suppose that it intends to do me good, since it comes in such a terrifying form, and therefore, as a prudent cow, I shall endeavor to escape from it." If you were to explain to this metaphysical ruminant that the train has no intention of leaving the rails, and is totally indifferent to the fate of the cow, the poor beast would be bewildered by anything so unnatural. The train that wishes her neither well nor ill would seem more cold and more abysmally horrifying than a train that wished her ill. Just this has happened with human beings. The course of nature brings them sometimes good fortune, sometimes evil. They cannot believe that this happens by accident. The cow, having known of a companion which had strayed on to the railway line and been killed by a train, would pursue her philosophical reflections, if she were endowed with that moderate degree of intelligence that characterizes most human beings, to the point of concluding that the unfortunate cow had been punished for sin by the god of the railway. She would be glad when his priests put fences along the line, and would warn younger and friskier cows never to avail themselves of accidental openings in the fence, since the wages of sin is death. By similar myths men have succeeded, without sacrificing their self-importance, in explaining many of the misfortunes to which they are subject. But sometimes misfortune befalls the wholly virtuous, and what are we to say in this case? We shall still be prevented by our feeling that we must be the center of the universe from admitting that misfortune has merely happened to us without anybody's intending it, and since we are not wicked by hypothesis, our misfortune must be due to somebody's malevolence, that is to say, to somebody wishing to injure us from mere hatred and not from the hope of any advantage to himself. It was this state of mind that gave rise to demonology, and the belief in witchcraft and black magic. The witch is a person who injures her neighbors from sheer hatred, not from any hope of gain. The belief in witchcraft, until about the middle of the seventeenth century, afforded a most satisfying outlet for the delicious emotion of self-righteous cruelty. There was Biblical warrant for the belief, since the Bible says: "Thou shalt not suffer a witch to live." And on this ground the Inquisition punished not only witches, but those who did not believe in the possibility of witchcraft, since to disbelieve it was heresy. Science, by giving some insight into natural causation, dissipated the belief in magic, but could not wholly dispel the fear and sense of insecurity that had given rise to it. In modern times, these same emotions find an outlet in fear of foreign nations, an outlet which, it must be confessed, requires not much in the way of superstitious support.

One of the most powerful sources of false belief is envy. In any small town you will find, if you question the comparatively well-to-do, that they all exaggerate their neighbors' incomes, which gives them an opportunity to justify an accusation of meanness. The jealousies of women are proverbial among men, but in any large office you will find exactly the same kind of jealousy among male officials. When one of them secures promotion the others will say: "Humph! So-and-so knows how to make up to the big men. I could have risen quite as fast as he has if I had chosen to debase myself by using the sycophantic arts of which he is not ashamed. No doubt his work has a flashy brilliance, but it lacks solidity, and sooner or later the authorities will find out their mistake." So all the mediocre men will say if a really able man is allowed to rise as fast as his abilities deserve, and that is why there is a tendency to adopt the rule of seniority, which, since it has nothing to do with merit, does not give rise to the same envious discontent.

One of the most unfortunate results of our proneness to envy is that it has caused a complete misconception of economic self-interest, both individual and national. I will illustrate by a parable. There was once upon a time a medium-sized town containing a number of butchers, a number of bakers, and so forth. One butcher, who was exceptionally energetic, decided that he would make much larger profits if all the other butchers were ruined and he became a monopolist. By systematically underselling them he succeeded in his object, though his losses meanwhile had almost exhausted his command of capital and credit. At the same time an energetic baker had had the same idea and had pursued it to a similar successful conclusion. In every trade which lived by selling goods to consumers the same thing had happened. Each of the successful monopolists had a happy anticipation of making a fortune, but unfortunately the ruined butchers were no longer in the position to buy bread, and the ruined bakers were no longer in the position to buy meat. Their employees had had to be dismissed and had gone elsewhere. The consequence was that, although the butcher and the baker each had a monopoly, they sold less than they had done in the old days. They had forgotten that while a man may be injured by his competitors he is benefited by his customers, and that customers become more numerous when the general level of prosperity is increased. Envy had made them concentrate their attention upon competitors and forget altogether the aspect of their prosperity that depended upon customers.

This is a fable, and the town of which I have been speaking never existed, but substitute for a town the world, and for individuals nations, and you will have a perfect picture of the economic policy universally pursued in the present day. Every nation is persuaded that its economic interest is opposed to that of every other nation, and that it must profit if other nations are reduced to destitution. During the First World War, I used to hear English people saying how immensely British trade would benefit from the destruction of German trade, which was to be one of the principal fruits of our victory. After the war, although we should have liked to find a market on the Continent of Europe, and although the industrial life of Western Europe depended upon coal from the Ruhr, we could not bring ourselves to allow the Ruhr coal industry to produce more than a tiny fraction of what it produced before the Germans were defeated. The whole philosophy of economic nationalism, which is now universal throughout the world, is based upon the false belief that the economic interest of one nation is necessarily opposed to that of another. This false belief, by producing international hatreds and rivalries, is a cause of war, and in this way tends to make itself true, since when war has once broken out the conflict of national interests becomes only too real. If you try to explain to someone, say, in the steel industry, that possibly prosperity in other countries might be advantageous to him, you will find it quite impossible to make him see the argument, because the only foreigners of whom he is vividly aware are his competitors in the steel industry. Other foreigners are shadowy beings in whom he has no emotional interest. This is the psychological root of economic nationalism, and war, and man-made starvation, and all the other evils which will bring our civilization to a disastrous and disgraceful end unless men can be induced to take a wider and less hysterical view of their mutual relations.

Another passion which gives rise to false beliefs that are politically harmful is pride—pride of nationality, race, sex, class, or creed. When I was young France was still regarded

as the traditional enemy of England, and I gathered as an un-
questionable truth that one Englishman could defeat three
Frenchmen. When Germany became the enemy this belief
was modified and English people ceased to mention derisively
the French propensity for eating frogs. But in spite of governmental efforts, I think few Englishmen succeeded in genuinely regarding the French as their equals. Americans and
Englishmen, when they become acquainted with the Balkans,
feel an astonished contempt when they study the mutual
enmities of Bulgarians and Serbs, of Hungarians and Ruma-
nians. It is evident to them that these enmities are absurd and
that the belief of each little nation in its own superiority has
no objective basis. But most of them are quite unable to see
that the national pride of a Great Power is essentially as unjustifiable as that of a little Balkan country.

Pride of race is even more harmful than national pride. When
I was in China I was struck by the fact that cultivated Chinese
were perhaps more highly civilized than any other human
beings that it has been my good fortune to meet. Nevertheless,
I found numbers of gross and ignorant white men who despised even the best of the Chinese solely because their skins
were yellow. In general, the British were more to blame in
this than the Americans, but there were exceptions. I was once
in the company of a Chinese scholar of vast learning, not only
of the traditional Chinese kind, but also of the kind taught in
Western universities, a man with a breadth of culture which
I scarcely hoped to equal. He and I went together into a garage
to hire a motor car. The garage proprietor was a bad type of
American, who treated my Chinese friend like dirt, contemp-
tuously accused him of being Japanese, and made my blood
boil by his ignorant malevolence. The similar attitude of the
English in India, exacerbated by their political power, was
one of the main causes of the friction that arose in that country between the British and the educated Indians. The superi-

ority of one race to another is hardly ever believed in for any good reason. Where the belief persists it is kept alive by military supremacy. So long as the Japanese were victorious, they entertained a contempt for the white man, which was the counterpart of the contempt that the white man had felt for them while they were weak. Sometimes, however, the feeling of superiority has nothing to do with military prowess. The Greeks despised the barbarians, even at times when the barbarians surpassed them in warlike strength. The more enlightened among the Greeks held that slavery was justifiable so long as the masters were Greek and the slaves barbarian, but that otherwise it was contrary to nature. The Jews had, in antiquity, a quite peculiar belief in their own racial superiority; ever since Christianity became the religion of the state Gentiles have had an equally irrational belief in their superiority to Jews. Beliefs of this kind do infinite harm, and it should be, but is not, one of the aims of education to eradicate them. I spoke a moment ago about the attitude of superiority that Englishmen have permitted themselves in their dealings with the inhabitants of India, which was naturally resented in that country, but the caste system arose as a result of successive invasions by "superior" races from the North, and is every bit as objectionable as white arrogance.

The belief in the superiority of the male sex, which has now officially died out in Western nations, is a curious example of the sin of pride. There was, I think, never any reason to believe in any innate superiority of the male, except his superior muscle. I remember once going to a place where they kept a number of pedigreed bulls, and what made a bull illustrious was the milk-giving qualities of his female ancestors. But if bulls had drawn up the pedigrees they would have been very different. Nothing would have been said about the female ancestors, except that they were docile and virtuous, whereas the male ancestors would have been celebrated for their supremacy in battle. In the case of cattle we can take a disinterested view of the relative merits of the sexes, but in the case of our own species we find this more difficult. Male superiority in former days was easily demonstrated, because if a woman questioned her husband's he could beat her. From superiority in this respect others were thought to follow. Men were more reasonable than women, more inventive, less swayed by their emotions, and so on. Anatomists, until the women had the vote, developed a number of ingenious arguments from the study of the brain to show that men's intellectual capacities must be greater than women's. Each of these arguments in turn was proved to be fallacious, but it always gave place to another from which the same conclusion would follow. It used to be held that the male foetus acquires a soul after six weeks, but the female only after three months. This opinion also has been abandoned since women have had the vote. Thomas Aquinas states parenthetically, as something entirely obvious, that men are more rational than women. For my part, I see no evidence of this. Some few individuals have some slight glimmerings of rationality in some directions, but so far as my observations go, such glimmerings are no commoner among men than among women.

Male domination has had some very unfortunate effects. It made the most intimate of human relations, that of marriage, one of master and slave, instead of one between equal partners. It made it unnecessary for a man to please a woman in order to acquire her as his wife, and thus confined the arts of courtship to irregular relations. By the seclusion which it forced upon respectable women it made them dull and uninteresting; the only women who could be interesting and adventurous were social outcasts. Owing to the dullness of respectable women, the most civilized men in the most civilized countries often became homosexual. Owing to the fact that there was no equality in marriage men became confirmed in domineering habits. All this has now more or less ended in civilized countries, but it will be a long time before either men or women learn to adapt their behavior completely to the new state of affairs. Emancipation always has at first certain bad effects; it leaves former superiors sore and former inferiors self-assertive. But it is to be hoped that time will bring adjustment in this matter as in others.

Another kind of superiority which is rapidly disappearing is that of class, which now survives only in Soviet Russia. In that country the son of a proletarian has advantages over the son of a bourgeois, but elsewhere such hereditary privileges are regarded as unjust. The disappearance of class distinctions is, however, far from complete. In America everybody is of opinion that he has no social superiors, since all men are equal, but he does not admit that he has no social inferiors, for, from the time of Jefferson onward, the doctrine that all men are equal applies only upwards, not downwards. There is on this subject a profound and widespread hypocrisy whenever people talk in general terms. What they really think and feel can be discovered by reading second-rate novels, where one finds that it is a dreadful thing to be born on the wrong side of the tracks, and that there is as much fuss about a *mésalliance* as there used to be in a small German Court. So long as great inequalities of wealth survive it is not easy to see how this can be otherwise. In England, where snobbery is deeply ingrained, the equalization of incomes which has been brought about by the war has had a profound effect, and among the young the snobbery of their elders has begun to seem somewhat ridiculous. There is still a very large amount of regrettable snobbery in England, but it is connected more with education and manner of speech than with income or with social status in the old sense.

Pride of creed is another variety of the same kind of feeling. When I had recently returned from China I lectured on that country to a number of women's clubs in America. There was always one elderly woman who appeared to be sleeping throughout the lecture, but at the end would ask me, somewhat portentously, why I had omitted to mention that the Chinese, being heathen, could of course have no virtues. I imagine that the Mormons of Salt Lake City must have had a similar attitude when non-Mormons were first admitted among them. Throughout the Middle Ages, Christians and Mohammedans were entirely persuaded of each other's wickedness and were incapable of doubting their own superiority.

All these are pleasant ways of feeling "grand." In order to be happy we require all kinds of supports to our self-esteem. We are human beings, therefore human beings are the purpose of creation. We are Americans, therefore America is God's own country. We are white, and therefore God cursed Ham and his descendants who were black. We are Protestant or Catholic, as the case may be, therefore Catholics or Protestants, as the case may be, are an abomination. We are male, and therefore women are unreasonable; or female, and therefore men are brutes. We are Easterners, and therefore the West is wild and woolly; or Westerners, and therefore the East is effete. We work with our brains, and therefore it is the educated classes that are important; or we work with our hands, and therefore manual labor alone gives dignity. Finally, and above all, we each have one merit which is entirely unique: we are Ourself. With these comforting reflections we go out to do battle with the world; without them our courage might fail. Without them, as things are, we should feel inferior because we have not learned the sentiment of equality. If we could feel genuinely that we are the equals of our neighbors, neither their betters nor their inferiors, perhaps life would become less of a battle, and we should need less in the way of intoxicating myth to give us Dutch courage.

One of the most interesting and harmful delusions to which

men and nations can be subjected is that of imagining themselves special instruments of the Divine Will. We know that
when the Israelites invaded the Promised Land it was they
who were fulfilling the Divine Purpose, and not the Hittites,
the Girgashites, the Amorites, the Canaanites, the Perizzites,
the Hivites, or the Jebusites. Perhaps if these others had
written long history books the matter might have looked a
little different. In fact, the Hittites did leave some inscriptions,
from which you would never guess what abandoned wretches
they were. It was discovered, "after the fact," that Rome was
destined by the gods for the conquest of the world. Then
came Islam with its fanatical belief that every soldier dying
in battle for the True Faith went straight to a Paradise more
attractive than that of the Christians', as houris are more attractive than harps. Cromwell was persuaded that he was the
Divinely appointed instrument of justice for suppressing Catholics and malignants. Andrew Jackson was the agent of Manifest Destiny in freeing North America from the incubus of
Sabbath-breaking Spaniards. In our day, the sword of the
Lord has been put into the hands of the Marxists. Hegel
thought that the Dialectic with fatalistic logic had given
supremacy to Germany. "No," said Marx, "not to Germany,
but to the Proletariat." This doctrine has kinship with the
earlier doctrines of the Chosen People and Manifest Destiny.
In its character of fatalism it has viewed the struggle of op-
ponets as one against destiny, and argued that therefore the
wise man would put himself on the winning side as quickly
as possible. That is why this argument is such a useful one
politically. The only objection to it is that it assumes a knowledge of the Divine purposes to which no rational man can lay
claim, and that in the execution of them it justifies a ruthless
cruelty which would be condemned if our program had a
merely mundane origin. It is good to know that God is on our
side, but a little confusing when you find the enemy equally

convinced of the opposite. To quote the immortal lines of the poet during the First World War:

> Gott strafe England, and God save the King.
> God this, and God that, and God the other thing.
> "Good God," said God, "I've got my work cut out."

Belief in a Divine mission is one of the many forms of certainty that have afflicted the human race. I think perhaps one of the wisest things ever said was when Cromwell said to the Scotch before the battle of Dunbar: "I beseech you in the bowels of Christ, think it possible that you may be mistaken." But the Scotch did not, and so he had to defeat them in battle. It is a pity that Cromwell never addressed the same remark to himself. Most of the greatest evils that man has inflicted upon man have come through people feeling quite certain about something which, in fact, was false. To know the truth is more difficult than most men suppose, and to act with ruthless determination in the belief that truth is the monopoly of their party is to invite disaster. Long calculations that certain evil in the present is worth inflicting for the sake of some doubtful benefit in the future are always to be viewed with suspicion, for, as Shakespeare says: "What's to come is still unsure." Even the shrewdest men are apt to be wildly astray if they prophesy so much as ten years ahead. Some people will consider this doctrine immoral, but after all it is the Gospel, which says "take no thought for the morrow."

In public, as in private life, the important thing is tolerance and kindliness, without the presumption of a superhuman ability to read the future.

Instead of calling this essay "Ideas That Have Harmed Mankind," I might perhaps have called it simply "Ideas Have Harmed Mankind," for, seeing that the future cannot be foretold and that there is an almost endless variety of possible beliefs about it, the chance that any belief which a man may hold may be true is very slender. Whatever you think is going to happen ten years hence, unless it is something like the sun rising tomorrow that has nothing to do with human relations, you are almost sure to be wrong. I find this thought consoling when I remember some gloomy prophecies of which I myself have rashly been guilty.

But you will say: how is statesmanship possible except on the assumption that the future can be to some extent foretold? I admit that some degree of prevision is necessary, and I am not suggesting that we are completely ignorant. It is a fair prophecy that if you tell a man he is a knave and a fool he will not love you, and it is a fair prophecy that if you say the same thing to seventy million people they will not love you. It is safe to assume that cut-throat competition will not produce a feeling of good fellowship between the competitors. It is highly probable that if two states equipped with modern armament face each other across a frontier, and if their leading statesmen devote themselves to mutual insults, the population of each side will in time become nervous, and one side will attack for fear of the other doing so. It is safe to assume that a great modern war will not raise the level of prosperity even among the victors. Such generalizations are not difficult to know. What is difficult is to foresee in detail the long-run consequences of a concrete policy. Bismarck with extreme astuteness won three wars and unified Germany. The long-run result of his policy has been that Germany has suffered two colossal defeats. These resulted because he taught Germans to be indifferent to the interests of all countries except Germany, and generated an aggressive spirit which in the end united the world against his successors. Selfishness beyond a point, whether individual or national, is not wise. It may with luck succeed, but if it fails failure is terrible. Few men will run this risk unless they are supported by a theory, for it is only theory that makes men completely incautious.

Passing from the moral to the purely intellectual point of view, we have to ask ourselves what social science can do in the way of establishing such causal laws as should be a help to statesmen in making political decisions. Some things of real importance have begun to be known, for example how to avoid slumps and large-scale unemployment such as afflicted the world after the last war. It is also now generally known by those who have taken the trouble to look into the matter that only an international government can prevent war, and that civilization is hardly likely to survive more than one more great war, if that. But although these things are known, the knowledge is not effective; it has not penetrated to the great masses of men, and it is not strong enough to control sinister interests. There is, in fact, a great deal more social science than politicians are willing or able to apply. Some people attribute this failure to democracy, but it seems to me to be more marked in autocracy than anywhere else. Belief in democracy, however, like any other belief, may be carried to the point where it becomes fanatical, and therefore harmful. A democrat need not believe that the majority will always decide wisely; what he must believe is that the decision of the majority, whether wise or unwise, must be accepted until such time as the majority decides otherwise. And this he believes not from any mystic conception of the wisdom of the plain man, but as the best practical device for putting the reign of law in place of the reign of arbitrary force. Nor does the democrat necessarily believe that democracy is the best system always and everywhere. There are many nations which lack the self-restraint and political experience that are required for the success of parliamentary institutions, where the democrat, while he would wish them to acquire the necessary political education, will recognize that it is useless to thrust upon them prematurely a system which is almost certain to break down. In politics, as elsewhere, it does not do to deal in absolutes; what is good in one time and place may be bad in another, and what satisfies the political instincts of one nation may to another seem wholly futile. The general aim of the democrat is to substitute government by general assent for government by force, but this requires a population that has undergone a certain kind of training. Given a nation divided into two nearly equal portions which hate each other and long to fly at each other's throats, the portion which is just less than half will not submit tamely to the domination of the other portion, nor will the portion which is just more than half show, in the moment of victory, the kind of moderation which might heal the breach.

The world at the present day stands in need of two kinds of things. On the one hand, organization—political organization for the elimination of wars, economic organization to enable men to work productively, especially in the countries that have been devastated by war, educational organization to generate a sane internationalism. On the other hand it needs certain moral qualities—the qualities which have been advocated by moralists for many ages, but hitherto with little success. The qualities most needed are charity and tolerance, not some form of fanatical faith such as is offered to us by the various rampant isms. I think these two aims, the organizational and the ethical, are closely interwoven; given either the other would soon follow. But, in effect, if the world is to move in the right direction it will have to move simultaneously in both respects. There will have to be a gradual lessening of the evil passions which are the natural aftermath of war, and a gradual increase of the organizations by means of which mankind can bring each other mutual help. There will have to be a realization at once intellectual and moral that we are all one family, and that the happiness of no one branch of this family can be built securely upon the ruin of another. At the present time, moral defects stand in the way of clear thinking, and muddled thinking encourages moral defects. Perhaps, though I scarcely dare to hope it, the hydrogen bomb will terrify mankind into sanity and tolerance. If this should happen we shall have reason to bless its inventors.

XI

Eminent Men I Have Known

I HAVE known in the course of my life many eminent men and women, from Victorian times to the present day. The quality of being unforgettable, or personally impressive, has not, in my experience, been greatest in those who have made the greatest mark in history, except in a few cases. My only encounter with Queen Victoria was at the age of two, and unfortunately I do not remember it, but my elders noted with surprise that my behavior was quite respectful. On the other hand, it was at the same age that I first met Robert Browning, whom many considered the best poet of his age; I interrupted his discourse by saying in a piercing voice "I wish that man would stop talking." I met him frequently in the last years of his life, and found nothing in him to command reverence. He was a pleasant, kindly old gentleman, very much at home at tea-parties of middle-aged ladies, dapper, suave, and thoroughly domesticated, but without the divine fire that one expects of a poet.

On the other hand, Tennyson, whom I also saw frequently, was always acting the poet, and incurred my adolescent scorn on that account. He used to stalk about the countryside in a flowing Italian cloak, very emphatically not seeing the people he happened to meet, and displaying the behavior appropriate to poetic abstraction. Of the other poets I have met, I think the most unforgettable was Ernst Toller, chiefly through his capacity for intense impersonal suffering. Rupert Brooke, whom I knew fairly well, was beautiful and vital, but the impression was marred by a touch of Byronic insincerity and by a certain flamboyance.

Among eminent philosophers, excluding men still alive, the most personally impressive, to me, was William James. This was in spite of a complete naturalness and absence of all apparent consciousness of being a great man. No degree of democratic feeling and of desire to identify himself with the common herd could make him anything but a natural aristocrat, a man whose personal distinction commanded respect. Some philosophers—not necessarily the ablest—are impressive through their quality of intellectual honesty. Of these a very good example was Henry Sidgwick, who was my teacher in ethics. In his youth fellowships at Cambridge were only open to those who would sign the Thirty-Nine Articles of the Church of England. Years after he had signed them, he developed doubts, and, though not expected to affirm that his beliefs remained unchanged, decided that it was his duty to resign. This action hastened the change in the law which put an end to the old theological restrictions. As a teacher, he showed the same honesty, and considered objections by pupils as courteously and carefully as if they had been made by colleagues. This made his teaching more fruitful than that of many abler men.

Men of science, at their best, have a special kind of impressiveness, resulting from the combination of great intellect with childlike simplicity. When I say "simplicity," I do not mean anything involving lack of cleverness; I mean the habit of thinking impersonally, without regard for the worldly advantage or disadvantage of an opinion or an action. Among the men of science I have known, Einstein is a supreme example of this quality.

Coming to politicians, I have known seven Prime Ministers, from my grandfather (who was Prime Minister in 1846) to Mr. Attlee. Far the most unforgettable of those was Gladstone, whom those who knew him always alluded to as "Mr." Gladstone. The only other man known to me in public life that I could regard as his equal in personal impressiveness was Lenin. Mr. Gladstone was embodied Victorianism; Lenin was embodied Marxian formulas—neither quite human, but each with the power of a natural force.

Mr. Gladstone, in private life, dominated by the power of his eye, which was quick and piercing, and calculated to inspire terror. One felt, like a small boy in presence of an old-fashioned schoolmaster, a constant impulse to say "please, Sir, it wasn't me." Everybody felt like this. I cannot imagine a human being who would have ventured to tell him a story even in the faintest degree *risqué;* his moral horror would have frozen the narrator to stone. I had a grandmother who was the most formidable woman I have ever known; other eminent men invariably quailed before her. But once, when Mr. Gladstone was coming to tea, she told us all in advance that she was going to set him right on his Irish policy, of which she strongly disapproved. He came, and I was present throughout, waiting breathlessly for the expected clash. Alas! my grandmother was all softness, and said not a syllable to start the lion roaring; no one could have guessed that she disagreed with him about anything.

Far the most terrifying experience of my life was connected with Mr. Gladstone. When I was seventeen, a very shy and awkward youth, he came to stay with my family for the weekend. I was the only "man" in the house, and after dinner, when the ladies retired, I was left *tête-à-tête* with the ogre. I was

too petrified to perform my duties as a host, and he did nothing
to help me out. For a long time we sat in silence; at last, in his
booming bass voice, he condescended to make his one and only
remark: "This is very good port they've given me, but why
have they given it me in a claret glass?" Since then I have
faced infuriated mobs, angry judges, and hostile governments,
but never again have I felt such terror as in that searing moment.

Profound moral conviction was the basis of Mr. Gladstone's
political influence. He had all the skill of a clever politician, but
was sincerely convinced that every one of his maneuvers was
inspired by the most noble purposes. Labouchère, who was a
cynic, summed him up in the saying: "Like every politician, he
always has a card up his sleeve; but unlike the others, he thinks
the Lord put it there." Invariably he earnestly consulted his
conscience, and invariably his conscience earnestly gave him
the convenient answer.

The force of his personality is illustrated by the story—true
or false—of his encounter with a drunken man at a meeting.
This man, it appears, was of the opposite political party, and
interrupted frequently. At last Mr. Gladstone fixed him with
his eye, and spake these words: "*May I request the gentleman
who has, not once but repeatedly, interrupted my observations
by his interjections, to extend to me that large measure of
courtesy which, were I in his place and he in mine, I should
most unhesitatingly extend to him.*" It is said—and I can well
believe it—that the man was sobered by the shock, and remained silent the rest of the evening.

Oddly enough, about half of his compatriots, including a
great majority of the well-to-do, regarded him as either mad
or wicked or both. When I was a child, most of the children I
knew were conservatives, and they solemnly assured me, as a
well-known fact, that Mr. Gladstone ordered twenty top-hats
from various hatters every morning, and that Mrs. Gladstone

had to go round after him and disorder them. (This was before the days of telephones.) Protestants supposed him secretly in league with the Vatican; the rich regarded him (with few exceptions) as Mr. Roosevelt was regarded by the most reactionary of the American rich. But he remained serene, because he never doubted that the Lord was on his side. And to half the nation he was almost a god.

Lenin, with whom I had a long conversation in Moscow in 1920, was, superficially, very unlike Gladstone, and yet, allowing for the difference of time and place and creed, the two men had much in common. To begin with the differences: Lenin was cruel, which Gladstone was not; Lenin had no respect for tradition, whereas Gladstone had a great deal; Lenin considered all means legitimate for securing the victory of his party, whereas for Gladstone politics was a game with certain rules that must be observed. All these differences, to my mind, are to the advantage of Gladstone, and accordingly Gladstone on the whole had beneficent effects, while Lenin's effects were disastrous. In spite of all these dissimilarities, however, the points of resemblance were quite as profound. Lenin supposed himself to be an atheist, but in this he was mistaken. He thought that the world was governed by the dialectic, whose instrument he was; just as much as Gladstone, he conceived of himself as the human agent of a superhuman Power. His ruthlessness and unscrupulousness were only as to means, not as to ends; he would not have been willing to purchase personal power at the expense of apostasy. Both men derived their personal force from this unshakable conviction of their own rectitude. Both men, in support of their respective faiths, ventured into realms in which, from ignorance, they could only cover themselves with ridicule—Gladstone in Biblical criticism, Lenin in philosophy.

Of the two, I should say that Gladstone was the more unforgettable as a personality. I take as the test what one would have

thought of each if one had met him in a train without knowing who he was. In such circumstances Gladstone, I am convinced, would have struck me as one of the most remarkable
men I had ever met, and would have soon reduced me to a
speechless semblance of agreement. Lenin, on the contrary,
might, I think, have seemed to me at once a narrow-minded
fanatic and a cheap cynic. I do not say that this judgment
would have been just; it would have been unjust, not positively,
but by what it would have omitted. When I met Lenin, I
had much less impression of a great man than I had expected;
my most vivid impressions were of bigotry and Mongolian
cruelty. When I put a question to him about socialism in agriculture, he explained with glee how he had incited the poorer
peasants against the richer ones, "and they soon hanged them
from the nearest tree—ha! ha! ha!" His guffaw at the thought
of those massacred made my blood run cold.

The qualities which make a political leader were less obvious
in Lenin than in Gladstone. I doubt whether he could have
become a leader in quieter times. His power depended upon
the fact that, in a bewildered and defeated nation, he, almost
alone, had no doubt, and held out hopes of a new sort of victory in spite of military disaster. He seemed to demonstrate
his gospel by cold reasoning, which invoked logic as his ally.
In this way the passion of his followers came to appear, to them
as to him, to have the sanction of science, and to be the very
means by which the world was to be saved. Robespierre must
have had something of the same quality.

I have spoken of men who were eminent in one way or
another. But in actual fact I have been quite as often impressed
by men and women of no eminence. What I have found most
unforgettable is a certain kind of moral quality, a quality of
self-forgetfulness, whether in private life, in public affairs, or
in the pursuit of truth. I had at one time a gardener who could
neither read nor write, but was a perfect type of simple good-

ness, such as Tolstoy loved to depict among peasants. A man whom, on account of his purity of heart, I shall never forget, was E. D. Morel. As a shipping clerk in Liverpool, he became aware of the horrors in King Leopold's exploitation of the Congo. In order to make his knowledge public, he had to sacrifice his position and means of livelihood. Single-handed at first, he gradually, in spite of opposition from all the governments of Europe, roused public opinion and compelled reform. The new consideration which he had thus won for himself he sacrificed to pacifism in the war, during the course of which he was sent to prison. He lived until shortly after the formation of the first Labor Government, from which Ramsay MacDonald excluded him in the hope of causing his own pacifist past to be overlooked. Worldly success seldom comes to such men, but they inspire love and admiration, in those who know them, surpassing what is given to those who are less pure of heart.

XII

Obituary*

(1937)

B Y the death of the Third Earl Russell (or Bertrand Russell, as he preferred to call himself) at the age of ninety, a link with a very distant past is severed. His grandfather, Lord John Russell, the Victorian Prime Minister, visited Napoleon in Elba; his maternal grandmother was a friend of the Young Pretender's widow. In his youth he did work of importance in mathematical logic, but his eccentric attitude during the First World War revealed a lack of balanced judgment which increasingly infected his later writings. Perhaps this is attributable, at least in part, to the fact that he did not enjoy the advantages of a public school education, but was taught at home by tutors until the age of 18, when he entered Trinity College, Cambridge, becoming 7th Wrangler in 1893 and a Fellow in 1895. During the fifteen years that followed, he produced the books upon which his reputation in the learned world was based: *The Foundations of Geometry, The Philosophy of Leibniz, The Principles of Mathematics*, and (in

* This obituary will (or will not) be published in *The Times* for June 1, 1962, on the occasion of my lamented but belated death. It was printed prophetically in *The Listener* in 1937.

collaboration with Dr. A. N. Whitehead) *Principia Mathematica*. The last work, which was of great importance in its day, doubtless owed much of its superiority to Dr. (afterwards Professor) Whitehead, a man who, as his subsequent writings showed, was possessed of that insight and spiritual depth so notably absent in Russell; for Russell's argumentation, ingenious and clever as it is, ignores those higher considerations that transcend mere logic.

This lack of spiritual depth became painfully evident during the First World War, when Russell, although (to do him justice) he never minimized the wrong done to Belgium, perversely maintained that, war being an evil, the aim of statesmanship should have been to bring the war to an end as soon as possible, which would have been achieved by British neutrality and a German victory. It must be supposed that mathematical studies had caused him to take a wrongly quantitative view which ignored the question of principle involved. Throughout the war, he continued to urge that it should be ended, on no matter what terms. Trinity College, very properly, deprived him of his lectureship, and for some months of 1918 he was in prison.

In 1920 he paid a brief visit to Russia, whose government did not impress him favorably, and a longer visit to China, where he enjoyed the rationalism of the traditional civilization, with its still surviving flavor of the eighteenth century. In subsequent years his energies were dissipated in writings advocating socialism, educational reform, and a less rigid code of morals as regards marriage. At times, however, he returned to less topical subjects. His historical writings, by their style and their wit, conceal from careless readers the superficiality of the antiquated rationalism which he professed to the end.

In the Second World War he took no public part, having escaped to a neutral country just before its outbreak. In private conversation he was wont to say that homicidal lunatics were well employed in killing each other, but that sensible men would keep out of their way while they were doing it. Fortunately this outlook, which is reminiscent of Bentham, has become rare in this age, which recognizes that heroism has a value independent of its utility. True, much of what was once the civilized world lies in ruins; but no right-thinking person can admit that those who died for the right in the great struggle have died in vain.

His life, for all its waywardness, had a certain anachronistic consistency, reminiscent of that of the aristocratic rebels of the early nineteenth century. His principles were curious, but, such as they were, they governed his actions. In private life he showed none of the acerbity which marred his writings, but was a genial conversationalist and not devoid of human sympathy. He had many friends, but had survived almost all of them. Nevertheless, to those who remained he appeared, in extreme old age, full of enjoyment, no doubt owing, in large measure, to his invariable health, for politically, during his last years, he was as isolated as Milton after the Restoration. He was the last survivor of a dead epoch.

ABOUT THE AUTHOR

BERTRAND ARTHUR WILLIAM RUSSELL *received the Nobel Prize for literature in 1950. He is the grandson of Lord John Russell, the British Foreign Secretary during the Civil War. Before going to Cambridge he was educated at home by governesses and tutors, acquiring a thorough knowledge of German and French; and it has been said that his "admirable and lucid English style may be attributed to the fact that he did not undergo a classical education at a public school." Certainly, this style is perceptible in the many books that have flowed from his pen during half a century—books that have shown him to be the most profound of mathematicians, the most brilliant of philosophers, and the most lucid of popularizers. His last major works were* A History of Western Philosophy, *published in 1945;* Human Knowledge: Its Scope and Limits, *published in 1948; and* Authority and the Individual, *published in 1949.*